SHAKESPEARE: OF AN AGE AND FOR ALL TIME

The Yale Shakespeare Festival Lectures

AMS PRESS
NEW YORK

SHAKESPEARE: OF AN AGE AND FOR ALL TIME

The Yale Shakespeare Festival Lectures

Charles Tyler Prouty, Editor

The Shoe String Press, 1954

Library of Congress Cataloging in Publication Data

Yale University. Yale Shakespeare Festival, 1954.
   Shakespeare: of an age and for all time.

   1. Shakespeare, William, 1564-1616--Addresses,
essays, lectures. 2. Shakespeare, William, 1564-1616--
Anniversaries, etc., 1954. I. Prouty, Charles Tyler,
ed. II. Title.
[PR2923.Y3 1973]   822.3'3   72-960
ISBN 0-404-05146-4

From the edition of 1954, Hamden
First AMS edition published in 1973
Manufactured in the United States of America

AMS PRESS INC.
NEW YORK, N.Y. 10003

CONTENTS

Charles Tyler Prouty

THE YALE SHAKESPEARE FESTIVAL

"Reade him, therefore; and
againe and againe: And if then
you do not like him, surely
you are in some manifest
danger, not to understand
him. "

--John Heminge and Henrie
Condell: "To the great
Variety of Readers. "
The First Folio, 1623.

February & March, 1954

The Yale Shakespeare Festival really began in May 1953 when Mr. McMullan, Mr. Kökeritz and I had luncheon together in Calhoun College. Mr. Kökeritz's book, Shakespeare's Pronunciation, had just been published and we were all fascinated with Shakespeare's spoken language as there revealed. A logical next step was to hear a whole play as originally spoken, an idea which interested Mr. McMullan and to which he promised his full support. The best time for such a production would, of course, have been during the week of April 23rd, the anniversary of Shakespeare's birth, but the schedule of the Department of Drama called for a major production in February with a final matinée on Alumni Day, February 22nd.

As we ended our luncheon matters were still in a highly exploratory state: the Department of Drama would have to be persuaded to approve and we could envision many objections. As I thought about the project that afternoon, my mind wandered in several directions when suddenly I realized that the first volumes of the revised Yale Shakespeare, on which Mr. Kökeritz and I had been working as general editors would be published in the spring of 1954 and that the Yale Press was planning publication, at about the same time, of a facsimile of the First Folio of 1623, the first collected edition of Shakespeare's plays and our only source for the texts of about half of them. As well, the Press was publishing a book of mine dealing with the highly controversial problem of Shakespeare's revision of old plays.

It seemed to me that we had good cause to signalize

3

PROUTY

Yale's contribution to the study of Shakespeare and the
Elizabethans. In the last six years the Press had published some fifteen books in this field, the majority by
members of Yale's English Department. In 1953 the
discovery of plans and records of the earliest Tudor
playhouse had been announced and a model of Trinity
Hall had been unveiled in the Yale Library. In the summer of 1953 the Library had acquired a Restoration
manuscript of Macbeth which promised, and has since
revealed, very important information as to Shakespeare's
text. The Libraries of both the School of Music and the
School of Law had recently acquired important manuscripts of the period and scholars in those schools had
published valuable contributions to Elizabethan and Renaissance studies. The Department of Drama through
its faculty and graduate students had recently demonstrated how much the history of the theatre means to our
understanding of dramatic literature. It was, I think,
the cumulative effect of all these factors which led me to
conceive of a Yale Shakespeare Festival combining a lecture series with the Yale Press publications, a performance of a play in the original pronunciation and exhibitions in the library.

Early in June I discussed the idea with Mr. Holden,
Secretary of the University, who then gave and continued
to give his enthusiastic and whole-hearted support to the
project. With the beginning of term in September Mr.
Holden secured the consent of the University Committee
on Lectures to financial support of the lecture series.
At this time the theme of the Festival had been decided
upon: SHAKESPEARE: OF AN AGE AND FOR ALL
TIME. After completing this factual account of the Festival, I shall return to a discussion of this theme.

Returning to the chronological story we find things
happening in rapid succession. First the Department of
Drama, with some persuasion, decided to present The
Merry Wives of Windsor with the original pronunciation
under the direction of Mr. McMullan with coaching in
speech by Mr. Kökeritz. The Yale Dramat joined with
its space-fiction version of The Tempest and the scope

4

THE YALE SHAKESPEARE FESTIVAL

of the Festival widened. The Schools of Music, Medicine, and Law planned exhibitions, as did the University Art Gallery. The Friends of Music at Yale conceived of a concert of Elizabethan Music both vocal and instrumental using instruments of the period. Unfortunately the final arrangements for this concert were not settled until after the official program had gone to press, so notice had to be supplied with an insert. A third play was added when Berkeley College advanced the date of its annual Elizabethan play so that it would fall within the Festival period. Those who saw The Shoemakers' Holiday realize how well this farce comedy by one of Shakespeare's fellow dramatists rounded out the program.

Needless to say all this was not accomplished without many meetings of the interested parties under the guidance of Mr. Holden, Mr. Banks of the Yale News Bureau, and myself. At one of these meetings in December, Mr. Cole of the Department of Drama told the group of a call he had had from Paul Feigay, a graduate of the Department of Drama, and associate producer of the Omnibus Television program. Feigay was interested to know what the Department was doing in February that might be used for Omnibus. Of course the Festival was a natural for that program, but knowing the uncertainties of show business we all kept our fingers crossed for the next six or seven weeks until we received definite word from Mr. Feigay. In the interval various groups of the Omnibus staff came to New Haven to discuss the program; Mr. Banks went to New York to see Mr. Feigay; and Mr. Cole was on the telephone.

Early in the fall we had planned to invite a special audience to the first performance of The Merry Wives on Monday February 15th and to move Mr. McMullan's lecture to that day so that guests from out of town could attend both this lecture and the performance. The Elizabethan Club, which had already, through the good offices of its Librarian, Mr. Troxell, agreed to furnish the crown jewels of the library exhibition, its superb collection of Shakespeare quartos, offered to open the Club in a reception for the invited guests.

5

PROUTY

The invitation list was designed to include theatrical and academic people interested in Shakespeare, with schools as well as colleges and universities represented. The Yale Press as part of its contribution to the Festival asked Carl Rollins, sometime printer to the University, to design the invitation and the official program. The program, a fine example of typography contained the full list of events, three short essays on "The Shakespeare Festival", "Shakespeare and the Department of Drama", and "Shakespeare and the Undergraduate", as well as a list of all books on Shakespeare and the Elizabethans printed by the Yale Press.

As the first of February drew near the pace quickened. The material for the various exhibitions was gathered and here again the cooperation of the various branches and members of the University was a dominating factor. Mr. Kilgour of the School of Medicine and Mr. Thorne of the Law School arranged exhibitions in their respective libraries and in the Sterling Library as well. Mr. Shepard of the Music School exhibited only in Sterling, for want of room in Sprague Hall. Mr. Carroll of the Press arranged exhibits in both Sterling and the Memorial Room of the Yale Press. Mr. Laurson of the Department of Civil Engineering did an exhibition of science in Shakespeare's day. Mr. Fuller, Mr. Vietor, Miss Simonson and Miss Wynne of the University Library gathered books and planned the main exhibition. A set of all four folios was loaned by Mr. Pearson and the Elizabethan Club loaned its priceless quartos. Finally Mr. Osborn exhibited the treasures of his manuscript collection.

Originally Mr. Osborn had planned to loan two manuscripts to illustrate other exhibitions but on Sunday afternoon January 31st, the most interesting single feature of the various exhibitions came into being. As Mr. Osborn and I were searching through his manuscripts, we kept coming across things that ought to be shown, and then and there Mr. Osborn decided to exhibit some twenty-five of his most important manuscripts. From a news point of view Rafe Rabbard's Book of Inventions

6

THE YALE SHAKESPEARE FESTIVAL

with its colored drawing of an Elizabethan frogman
breathing through a schnorkle device received most attention. The London _Times_ carried two stories about
this, with the second being an account of the entire manuscript exhibition and emphasizing its important as well
as its sensational features.

Three days later the first lecture was given in Strath-
cona Auditorium by Mr. Harding. Neither Mr. Holden
nor I expected the number of people who turned out.
About 700 tried to get in and of these 150 were turned
away. We decided to move the remaining lectures to the
larger auditorium of the Law School and even there the
successive audiences filled the hall long before the lectures began.

The various performances and the concert also played
to packed houses. There was standing room only for
every performance of The Merry Wives, The Tempest
grossed $5,000, Sprague Hall was completely filled for
the concert and the Great Hall of Berkeley was packed
for both performances. Over 9,000 people visited the
exhibition at the Art Gallery and it is estimated that some
25,000 people visited one or another of the various features of the Festival.

The opening night of The Merry Wives was a festive
affair with a large number of guests from New York and
New England. Of prime interest, to the cast in particular, was the presence in the audience of Mr. Brooks
Atkinson of the New York Times. His review of the play
which appeared on Wednesday morning was a great pleasure to us all for Mr. Atkinson had enjoyed, "Quite a
cheerful evening."

On Friday, the 19th, chaos came to the University
Theatre: some 100 technicians brought from New York
six television cameras, miles of cables and mountains
of equipment, but order soon appeared under the guiding
hand of Mr. Delbert Mann, a graduate of the Department
of Drama in 1948 and a leading director for the National
Broadcasting Company who was loaned to the Columbia
Broadcasting System for this particular show.

The first problem for Mr. Alistair Cooke, Mr. Köker-

7

itz, Mr. McMullan and me was the script of the show.
The working script had been prepared first by Mr. Hugh
Hill who graduated last June from the Department of
Drama. This had been reworked by the Omnibus staff in
New York, but it was obviously too long as we learned on
our first run through. The total number of times we ran
through this first part of the show with Mr. Cooke inter-
viewing the three of us is lost in my memory but it seems
now that I did little else from Friday until the show was
over at 6:30 P.M. on Sunday. When I was not rehearsing,
Mr. Richardson, who appeared with me in the opening of
the program, and I were guarding the books and manuscripts which he and I had brought over from the library.
We had two Shakespeare folios, two quartos and two manuscripts as well as other books which Omnibus had in-
sured for $70,000. On Sunday, since we were to be in the
theatre all day, we had a campus policeman locked up in
an office with the books when they were not actually being
used for rehearsal.

By Sunday afternoon we were ready for a dress rehearsal with cameras on and the show being sent over the
coaxial cable to New York to test facilities and to get the
reactions of the staff in New York. Then after a few min-
or changes we were set for the big moment of going on
the air and showing the Yale Shakespeare Festival to some
17,000,000 people across the breadth of America. Mr.
Cooke did his usual polished job and kept the program
spontaneous by varying his questions and comments. At
one point, for example, he asked me to explain what a
folio is. This question had been cut from the script Friday night and had not been used on Saturday or Sunday.
Suddenly when we were on the air he put it back in. Fortunately I grabbed a piece of paper and explained the
printing and folding of a folio sheet. Then in a moment
it was all over and Mr. Cooke had left the greenroom for
backstage to talk with Mr. Kökeritz about pronunciation
and puns. He next went onstage where Mr. McMullan
was rehearsing some of the cast. Finally the audience
saw and heard two scenes from the play itself and Mr.
Cooke in a final shot bade "Goodbye from Yale Univarsity"

THE YALE SHAKESPEARE FESTIVAL

to which institution he had been graciously welcomed by President A. Whitney Griswold.

The next week saw The Tempest performed in a setting and costumes of the future--the world of space men. Truly the Festival had taken Shakespeare from the days of Elizabeth across the centuries to the future and Shakespeare had been seen as the great dramatist "of an age and for all time. "

These words are a variation of a line from Ben Jonson's tribute which appeared in the prefatory matter of the First Folio of 1623. The poem entitled "To the memory of my beloved, The Author Mr. William Shakespeare: And what he hath left us" reads in part:

> Triumph, my Britain, thou hast one to showe,
> To whom all scenes of Europe homage owe,
> He was not of an age, but for all time!

This vaunt clearly indicates Jonson's meaning: Shakespeare was the greatest dramatist of all time.

Another tribute to Shakespeare by a great poet is found in Milton's "L'Allegro" where we read:

> Then to the well-trod stage anon,
> If Jonson's learned sock be on,
> Or sweetest Shakespeare, Fancy's child,
> Warble his native wood-notes wild.

This view of Jonson as learned and Shakespeare as a rather untutored native genius persisted through the 17th century; but with the 18th the work of the scholars began and has continued ever since, with the result that we today know more about Shakespeare and his plays than has any age save his own, and that age we have come to know intimately.

To assess our accumulated knowledge has been one aim of these Festival lectures, for the more completely we understand that world ruled over by Queen Elizabeth and King James the better we can understand the plays as creations of an age, but with those eternal values which

9

have spoken to the souls and hearts of men in all ages.
Mr. Harding illustrated this in several ways. The extent
of the formal education of the audience, for example, im-
presses upon us their response to the classical references, to the rhetorical patterns, and the imagery of the
poetry. A whole series of lectures could be given on the
basic assumptions of the Elizabethans on such subjects
as religion, government, economics, the social order
and even literature itself, but our purpose was to survey
an even larger area and so Mr. Kökeritz devoted himself
to that which is largely unexplored, the study of Shakespeare's language where so much remains to be done.

In the realm of the Elizabethan theatre much also remains to be done even though recent years have produced
new facts and many new theories. Here Mr. McMullan
showed us how a knowledge of Shakespeare's theatre en-
ables us to produce the plays in our own time, not with
the rigid pedantry of antiquarianism but with the spirit
of imagination and movement which originally animated
them.

Going back for understanding but always returning to
our own age, for the plays belong to us and to the future,
Mr. Richardson continued to exemplify the theme of the
Festival in his consideration of the neglected early history plays. Here in reworking the plays of other men
Shakespeare found a theme which was to run as a leit-
motiv through his plays and into our perception of the
world about us--What is the right course for a man to
follow in a world where the issues are never simple and
where men are motivated to action by many forces?

A vigorous portrayal of the course that leads to ruin
was shown to us by Mr. Waith in his picture of the black
evil that was Macbeth. The course that leads upward to
transcendent nobility was revealed by Mr. Pearson as
he led us along the ways that Antony and Cleopatra trav-
ersed to find that golden ring which binds them ever together in the hearts of men in this age and for all time.

Davis P. Harding

SHAKESPEARE THE ELIZABETHAN

"What, a play toward! I'll
be an auditor. "

--<u>Midsummer Night's
Dream</u> (3.1.81)

February 3, 1954

To admire the plays of Shakespeare and not to be curious about the audience for which such plays could have been written is almost a contradiction in terms. One ineluctable fact, it seems to me, we are bound to acknowledge at the outset. Shakespeare wrote for this Elizabethan audience and he wrote for no other audience. It is highly improbable that he ever consciously thought of himslef as writing his plays for posterity. On the contrary, it is likely that, for business or personal or even aesthetic reasons, he resented, as we know at least one other Elizabethan dramatist resented, the printing of his plays in quarto and tolerated the practice strictly as a defensive measure against unauthorized editions.

The fact that Shakespeare aimed his plays so exclusively at his contemporary audience cannot fail to lend it an intrinsic importance. It should make us initially distrustful of any theory based upon the notion that Shakespeare succeeded in spite of his audience--distrustful, for example, of such a position as that taken some years ago by the eminent English poet and critic, Robert Bridges:

> Shakespeare should not be put into the hands of the young without the warning that the foolish things in his plays are for the foolish, the filthy for the filthy, and the brutal for the brutal; and that, if out of veneration for his genius we are led to admire or even tolerate such things, we may be thereby not conforming ourselves to him, but only degrading ourselves to the level of his

13

audience, and learning contamination from those
wretched beings who can never be forgiven their
share in preventing the greatest poet and dramatist of the world from being the best artist.

In other words, to the extent that Shakespeare's genius
could be debauched, his audience debauched it--surely a
comforting doctrine for bardolaters. Yet I believe it is
true that this attitude toward Shakespeare's audience, at
least in a modified or attenuated form, is still the pre-
valent one today.

Let us assume that the year is 1600 or 1601 and that
you are in London with a free afternoon on your hands.
That you should have this free afternoon to yourself at
all is a little surprising. Working hours in Elizabethan
London were long--twelve hours in the summer and a
minimum of eight in dead winter--and the rules and reg-
ulations to enforce them were stringent. The chances are,
therefore, that this is a Sunday or holiday afternoon or
perhaps even a Saturday afternoon, if you are fortunate
enough to be employed in one of those crafts, like the
leather-workers, which knocked off work early on that
day. Of course, there was then, as there is now, a close
correlation between occupation and available leisure time.
A shopkeeper or a merchant or a gentleman or a law student at one of the Inns of Court or an idle housewife could
arrange for a free afternoon far more easily and plausibly
than handicraft workers or common laborers. But here
I must invoke the law of averages. You are probably a
craftsman or one of his numerous dependents. It has been
estimated that this economic group contributed pretty
close to fifty percent of the total adult population of London
at the turn of the century. I now come at once to a point
of some importance. If you belong to this economic group,
the chances are at least good that you have had a grammar
school education, or at least a substantial part of one. It
is a point I feel called upon to stress because you have so
often been accused of illiteracy.

According to A. F. Leach, the standard authority on
the subject, there were, before the Reformation, more

SHAKESPEARE THE ELIZABETHAN

boys attending grammar school in proportion to the population than there were in 1896, the date when he completed his study. Now it is true that the ill-conceived Chantries Act of 1548 dealt the cause of public school education in England a severe blow. In one way or another, this Act was responsible for the dissolution of many of the existing schools and the weakening of others. But with the accession of Elizabeth, the trend was reversed with a vengeance, until in 1581, Richard Mulcaster, one of the most famous schoolmasters of his time, reported that "during the time of Her Majesty's most fortunate reign, already, there hath been more schools erected than all the rest be that were before her time in the whole realm". Even so it is apparent that the schools were not able to keep pace with the mounting eagerness of parents to educate at least their male offspring. Mulcaster speaks of "this flocking multitude which will needs to school," of the "numbers and confusion" in schools, and of "the multitude which oppresseth learning with too, too many".

There are, of course, no statistics available for the number of boys attending grammar schools at the end of the sixteenth century, but one set of figures is revealing. These figures are from the records of the Stationers' Company. Only 1,250 copies of an ordinary book might be printed from the same set of type, but of Lily's Latin Grammar, the only authorized Latin grammar during the reign of Elizabeth and for long afterwards, four double impressions, or 10,000 copies, annually, were allowed to be printed. These figures are especially illuminating in view of the notorious tendency of schoolboys to keep used texts in circulation until they had been literally fingered and thumbed out of existence.

How are we to account for this accelerated demand for a grammar school education? Before the Reformation, again according to Leach, "it was the middle classes, whether country or town, the younger sons of the nobility or farmers, the lesser landholders, the prosperous tradesmen, who created a demand for education and furnished the occupants of Grammar Schools." But by the

15

end of the century it is apparent that the schools were
increasingly responding to the demands made upon them
by what might be termed the lower middle classes. Once
more let me quote Mulcaster. He writes of "the meaner
sort, whose children maintain schools most, and swarm
thickest in all places and professions." That was in 1581.
Two years earlier an anonymous educationalist wrote
tauntingly of "these common schools (whereof in England
there are many) that receive all sorts of children to be
taught, be their parents never so poor, and the boys
never so unapt." In 1596 Edward Coote, in an Elizabethan version of the modern "educate yourself at home" program, declares that his book, The English Schoolmaster,
will "ease the poorer sort of much charge that they have
been at, in maintaining their children long at school, and
in buying many books."

The chances are at least good, then, that you have
had a grammar school education, or at least part of one,
before proceeding to your apprenticeship at the age of
fourteen or fifteen. Later I shall attempt to assess the
importance of this assumption.

Now having, perhaps somewhat optimistically, provided you with a grammar school education, I shall return you to your dilemma--the challenge of your free
afternoon. What will you do with it? One factor which
will obviously carry a good deal of weight in influencing
your decision will be the amount of uncommitted money
you have currently in your pocket. Recalling your economic status, I will hazard the guess that it isn't much.

If you are a skilled workman or his assistant, you
are earning fifteen pennies a day, take or give a penny.
Since, out of its general economic context, such a figure
is meaningless, let me try to convert it into Elizabethan
purchasing power. There is an initial difficulty which I
should mention right away. During the whole period of
Shakespeare's active career as playwright in London,
prices showed a steady tendency to outdistance wages.
Although London craftsmen were better paid by about
thirty percent than craftsmen in other parts of the island,
in 1600 or 1601 you must have been hard put to make

both ends meet. The cost of clothes was especially pro-
hibitive. The diary of Philip Henslowe, the owner of the
Rose Theater, records expenditures of eighteen shillings
to a tailor for the making of a suit; he paid out another
twenty shillings for a woman's gray gown: that is, an
ordinary working dress. Philip Henslowe, it may be added, was a frugal man. Now you are making a little over
five shillings a week, and you have to feed your family
as well as clothe it. Here, therefore, are a few more
figures, based upon a scale of ceiling prices for food
established during the mobilization of August, 1599. Good
quality beef, 14d. for 8 pounds; cheese 1 1/2d. to 2d. pe
per pound; butter 4d. per pound; eggs, 2d. would buy you
seven; a fat pig, 16d; capons 20d. for two. Unless you
are a miser or a scoundrel it isn't likely that, at any
given moment during the week, you are going to have
more than a pittance to spend on commercialized pleasures.

We all know that, during periods of rising prices,
the costs of these pleasures rise, too. According to that
bumptious and colorful Elizabethan journalist and tavern-
haunter, Tom Nashe, the chief amusements which the
city offered were "gameing, following of harlots, drinking, or seeing a Playe". If Nashe's selection seems lim-
ited and of a rather special character, we must not let
the fact that we live in an age unrivalled for the scope
and variety of its commercialized entertainment make
us complacent. The vitality of the Elizabethans was not
so plentifully provided with outlets.

In the case of the first and second of these amusements, ignorance and not prudery compels me to silence.
The Mobilization of 1599 provides no ceiling prices for
either of them. The phrase "six-penny damnation" is
suggestive but scarcely definitive. About all that can be
said is that, in both instances, the adventurous spirit
was running the risk of involving himself in expenditures
he did not envisage at the outset. In this connection, perhaps I ought to mention the passion of Elizabethans for
bull and bear baitings and, on a somewhat less spectacular level, for cockfights. Although this passion is

generally ascribed to bloodlust and an inborn Elizabethan brutality, it is only fair to add that another motive made a marked contribution to the popularity of these sporting events. They functioned as a sort of Elizabethan equivalent of our modern parimutuel racetracks. Nobody had yet invented such modern refinements as form charts and the daily double--that is, as far as we know--but it is clear that a good deal of money changed hands at the conclusion of one of these contests. And, at least in one respect, the Elizabethans were distinctly abreast of our own times. In an era before the "saliva test" was thought of, it was a rare gamecock which went into action without a good liberal slug of brandy under its crop.

Suppose, however, you decide to spend the afternoon at an alehouse or tavern. Here we are on firmer ground, although again we cannot afford to ignore the variable. How much you spend will depend on how much you drink. If you have the earnings of a skilled craftsman and the capacity of a Falstaff, you have no business in the tavern at all. One recalls the itemized account which the Prince and Poins find in Falstaff's pocket after the latter has capped an "action" at the Boarshead Tavern by falling asleep.

> Item, A Capon. 2s2d
> Item, Sauce. 4d.
> Item, Sack, two gallons. 5s8d
> Item, Anchovies and sack
>   after supper 2s6d
> Item, bread. one half-penny

The two gallons of sack which Falstaff consumed before supper would in itself have called for an expenditure in excess of your weekly wages.

But even if your tastes in strong drink do not run to the Falstaffian extreme, an afternoon in the tavern is likely to prove expensive by your standards. Sack will be as far out of your financial range as top-shelf Scotch whiskey is out of the range of a school teacher today. In his Survey of 1603, we find the historian Stow writing:

18

SHAKESPEARE THE ELIZABETHAN

"Quaffing... is mightily encreased, though greatly qualified among the poorer sort, not of any holy abstinencie, but of meer necessitie, Ale and Beere being small, and Wines in price above their reach. " Very well then. If you are really flush, you can sit down to a quart of strong ale. That will cost you 4d. or one-fourth of your daily wage. It looks as if you had better settle for small beer, which will run you only a penny a quart.

Or, you can forego the small beer and spend the penny you would have paid for it by going to see a play performed at one of the public theaters.

Faced by the choice between a quart of small beer and going to see a play, which for a penny will provide you with a whole afternoon of entertainment, you ought not, in all good conscience, to hesitate. Even an occasional Puritan could be found who would concede, if hardpressed, that the devil drove harder bargains at the taverns than at the playhouses. Thus after condemning the theaters, the Puritan Joseph Wyburne is forced to an obviously reluctant conclusion: "notwithstanding, if we marke how young men spend the latter end of the day in gaming, drinking, whoring, it were better to tollerate Playes. " Tom Nashe, no Puritan, comes to the same conclusion for a slightly different reason. He is speaking of the confirmed Elizabethan "playboy-type".

> Faith, when Dice, Lust, and Drunkenesse, and
> all have dealt upon him, if there be never a
> Playe for him to goe too for his pennie, he sits
> melancholie in his Chamber, devising upon
> felonie or treason, and howe he may best exalt
> himselfe by mischiefe.

There is this afternoon, however, a special reason why you decide to go to the theater. You have seen a playbill on a city street-post announcing that a new play of Hamlet is going to open at the Globe Playhouse. A new play by the city's most successful, most money-making playwright is an exciting event--that is, for a very small percentage of the London citizenry. The

distressing fact is that Londoners stayed away from the
theaters in droves. From time to time various reasons
have been brought forward to account for this revulsion.
We have heard a good deal, for example, of the antipathy
of the Puritans to stage-plays. Here is one representa-
tive opinion from the pen of Henry Crosse:

> Now the common haunters are for the most part,
> the leawdest persons in the land, apt for pilferie,
> periurie, forgerie, or any rogories, the very
> scum, rascallitie, and baggage of the people,
> thieves, cutpurses, shifters, cousoners; brief-
> ly an uncleane generation, and spawne of vipers:
> must not here be good rule, where is such a
> broode of Hell-bred creatures? for a Play is
> like a sincke in a Towne, whereunto all the
> filth does runne: or a byle in the body that
> draweth all the ill humours unto it.

Much, too, has been made of the hostile attitude of the
city fathers, who had a horror of crowds, regarding them,
and quite rightly too, as potential centers of infection,
political as well as physical. Eventually, as we know,
the theaters were forced to take refuge outside the juris-
diction of the city in less desirable neighborhoods, whereupon they were immediately stigmatized by the Puritans
for the bad company they kept.

There is no doubt--let us concede the point--that
moral or religious scruples kept many Elizabethans from
the theaters. But let us not ignore a more powerful factor
still--lack of interest. Perhaps as much as seventy percent of the London adult population stayed away from
plays simply because they did not like plays. You represent a small minority--the shifting thirteen percent, approximately, which went weekly to the theater. Now for
some Londoners, obviously, an afternoon at the theater
must have been a rare treat. On the other hand, there
were the fashionable young idlers cut to the pattern of
Sir John Davies' estimable Fuscus.

SHAKESPEARE THE ELIZABETHAN

He's like a horse, which, turning round a mill,
Doth always in the self-same circle tread:
First, he doth rise at ten; and at eleven
He goes to Gyls, where he doth eate till one;
Then see a play till sixe, and sups at seven;
And after supper, straight to bed is gone;
And there till ten next day he doth remaine,
And then he dines, and sees a Comedy
And then he suppes, and goes to bed againe:
Thus round he runs without variety.

Obviously, you are no Fuscus; you have a job to take
care of.

But just a moment. We know from Henslowe's Diary
that it was customary for new plays to open on week-day
afternoons. The recorded gate-receipts prove that almost
any play would draw large crowds on Sundays and holidays
but that only a new play or a very popular old play could
draw well during the week. Hamlet is a new play. This
raises an embarrassing question which we may as well
ask at once and get it over with. Why aren't you at work?
The answer, I am afraid, is that you are playing hookey
from your job. There is more than one complaint about
you and your kind in the records of the City of London.
You are, in fact, one of the reasons why the theaters are
getting a bad name. I quote an entry in the Records for
the year 1597: "They [the theaters] maintaine idleness
in such persons as have no vocation & draw apprentices
and other servants from theire ordinary workes and all
sorts of people from the resort unto sermons and other
Christian exercises to the great hinderance of traides &
profanation of religion." It is not every man who can at
once be a threat to the economic order and to the established religion.

But it is too late to do anything about you now. You
are already on your way to the Globe Theater, knowing
that you must get there early to get any kind of satisfactory accomodations, or possibly even for that matter to
get inside the theater at all. This is a new play by

Shakespeare and, on the basis of past experience, you
are anticipating a capacity house. By the time you arrive
at the theater, after about a mile's walk, the pit is filling
up rapidly and, although for financial reasons, you had
originally expected to take up your station there, you now
reluctantly part with another penny in addition to the one
you paid at the door. I am here assuming that your decision to leave the pit was uncomplicated by other, less
creditable motives. For example, we have it on the good
authority of Stephen Gosson, that it had become "the
fashion of youthes to go first into the yarde, and to carry
theire eye through every gallery, then like unto ravens
where they spye the carion thither they flye, and presse
as nere to ye fairest as they can".

This second penny entitles you to a seat in the second
or third gallery. For you it is probably a reckless invest-
ment, and you may regret it later, but for the moment
you are well satisfied. You can see the whole theater from
where you are sitting and most of the people in it.

And what a hodge-podge of a crowd it is too! In a
few short years, it will vanish, and its like will not again
be seen in England. In the meantime, it will see, and
respond to, the greatest drama written in our language.
Is it altogether a coincidence that this drama and this
audience flourished together? And died out together? Let
us look at the audience a little more closely.

Perhaps the first thing about it to strike one would
be its size. In 1596, a visitor to London from Holland,
a certain Johannes de Witt, wrote it down that the Swan
Theater was capable of accomodating 3000 people in its
seats. Another visitor reckoned that the theaters in the
early nineties were "capable of many thousands." Until
quite recently, there was a tendency to discount these
estimates as exaggerations. But a few years ago, an
American scholar, Professor Alfred Harbage, after a
careful study of Henslowe's gate receipts and the architectural details of the building contract for the Fortune
Theater concluded that de Witt's estimate should not be
scaled down too much. His own estimate is that the

SHAKESPEARE THE ELIZABETHAN

Fortune Theater must have accomodated pretty close to 2500 people. Now we know that the Fortune Theater was closely modelled on the Globe. Since Hamlet was a new play, and since new plays generally drew capacity or near-capacity audiences, it is a fairly safe assumption that 2000 Londoners or more were present at the opening performance of Hamlet.

A good deal has been made of the noisy behavior of Elizabethans in the public theaters. At least in this respect, their bad manners must have been exaggerated. Now and then it is fair to apply common sense to some of our research problems. The noise-making potential of 2000 people would be quite high, and presumably the average Elizabethan, when he went to a play, expected to hear as well as see one. Unless the audience was reasonably quiet, he could scarcely have attained both objectives. Here the negative evidence assumes some importance. If unprejudiced theater-goers or the dramatists themselves had any complaints on this score, they have not survived. Yet we know the dramatists of the period were nothing if not critical of their audiences. They were not the sort to pass over a legitimate grievance in silence.

A second feature of this audience which could not fail to impress would be its democratic, heterogeneous character. This is in every sense of the word a true people's theater, like that of the ancient Greeks. Earlier in my discussion I sought to emphasize the fact that, of all the commercialized entertainment available in London at the turn of the century, the theater offered the cheapest, and by far the most for the money. Its penny admission-fee put it within economic reach of every Londoner. True, in view of the high cost of living, one would not perhaps expect the very poor to be present in large numbers. And probably they were not present in large numbers. But numerous contemporary references leave no doubt that the poorer classes were represented in the theater, and in at least considerable numbers. There is only one way of accounting for this anomaly, and I prefer

to let a contemporary of Shakespeare, Henry Crosse,
draw up the indictment.

> Nay many poore pincht, needie creatures, that
> live of almes, and that have scarce neither
> cloath to their backe, nor foode for the belley,
> yet wil make hard shift but they will see a Play,
> let wife & children begge, languish in penurie,
> and all they can rappe and rend, is little enough
> to lay upon such vanitie.

One must remember, however, that the penny dropped
in the collector's box, at a time when eggs were seven
for 2d., would not in any case have sufficed to keep the
wolf very far from the door.

Here in the theater-yard, the very poor would rub
elbows with the merely indigent and the decently frugal.
It is wrong to think of the so-called "penny stinkards" as
being a great, unwashed rabble. There were many respectable, educated Londoners who took up standing-
room in the yard for the same reasons which today prompt
school teachers to gravitate to the second balcony. How,
then, are we to account for the sneering and often savage
contempt which the dramatists of the period show for the
groundlings. It will be recalled that even Shakespeare,
or rather Hamlet, cannot resist taking a pot-shot in their
direction. For the most part, says Hamlet, the groundlings "are capable of nothing but inexplicable dumb-shows
and noise." I do not doubt that there were many people in
Shakespeare's audience to whom that unflattering description would apply. But it could not have applied to the
great majority, nor does Shakespeare--be it noted--so
apply it. On the contrary, the vogue for making contemp-
tuous references to the groundlings probably had its origin in an awareness of one of the facts of elementary
psychology. There is a touch of vanity in us all and, unless one is prepared to run the risk of being labelled a
mental groundling--no matter in what part of the theater
he happens to be standing or sitting--he had better remove the onus of suspicion by responding favorably to

the play before him. The dramatist is simply protecting
himself. In our own day, Shaw has delightfully revived
the custom of insulting his audience, extending however
the scope of the insult to include not just one sector of
his audience but all of it. We do not take offence because
we realize that the insult is not directed at us, but at the
mental groundlings who are sitting on either side of us.

At this opening performance of <u>Hamlet</u>, it may be
stated with confidence, every social and economic group
in Elizabethan London--from prince to pauper, from
courtier to gangster--would have been represented. There
would also have been a fair percentage of women in the
audience. Not many years ago it was generally assumed
that only a very few women attended plays and that, when
they did, they were motivated by concerns which, not by
any stretch of the imagination, could be labelled aesthetic.
Now, undoubtedly, women of a certain stamp would find
the theaters, with their predominantly male audiences,
ideal places in which to form quick and profitable friend-
ships. These women would assuredly have been present,
along with those other elements in the Elizabethan under-
world which operated most lucratively in large crowds
of people. Stephen Gosson, the most charming of the
Puritan writers who attacked the stage, may have been
prejudiced, but he was not given to mendacity. At the
theater, he says,

> you shall see suche heaving, and shooving, suche
> ytching and shouldring, too sitte by women; Suche
> care for their garments, that they bee not trode
> on: Such eyes to their lappes, that no chippes
> light in them: Such pillows to ther backes, that
> they take no hurte: Such masking in their eares,
> I knowe not what: Such giving them Pippins to
> passe the time: Suche playing at foote Saunt with-
> out Cardes: Such ticking, such toying, such
> smiling, such winking...that it is a right Comedie.

For Gosson, as he goes on to make clear, this can only
be the preamble to diversions of a less innocent nature.

But, Gosson and other Puritan writers notwithstanding,
it is certain that most of the women in the Elizabethan
audience were perfectly respectable: wives or sweet-
hearts, in the company of their men folk. For example,
Thomas Platter of Basle, who visited England in 1599,
comments, without disparagement, on the number of
women attending plays. And the backward devils do not
instigate every flirtation, even in a theater.

The presence of women in the Elizabethan audience
is another striking proof of its democratic character. It
is important to remember that no age ever cultivated its
class distinctions, and even distinctions within classes,
more assiduously than the Elizabethans. Listen to Thomas
Thomas Nashe:

> In London, the ritch disdayne the poore. The
> Courtier the Citizen. The Citizen the Countri-
> man. One Occupation disdayneth another. The
> Merchant the Retayler. The Retayler the Crafts-
> man. The better sort of Craftsman the baser.
> The Shoemaker the Cobler. The Cobler the Car-
> man, etc.

But it was not so in the theaters. The public theater, if
it did not exactly break down these distinctions, at least
for the duration of a performance held them in abeyance.
Listen now to Nashe's friend, Dekker, who complains
because the theater

> is so free in entertainment, allowing a stoole as
> well to the Farmers sonne as to your Templer:
> that your Stinckard has the selfe-same libertie
> to be there in his Tobacco-Fumes, which your
> sweet Courtier hath: and that your Car-man and
> Tinker claime as strong a voice in their suf-
> frage, and sit to give judgement on the plaies
> life and death, as well as the prowdest Momus
> among the tribe of Critick.

To apply Falstaff's words in another context, men of all

SHAKESPEARE THE ELIZABETHAN

sorts must have taken a pride in girding at Shakespeare.
It was probably the best thing that could have happened
to him.

Of this heterogeneous audience, I should guess that
about half had received a grammar school education.
This estimate, I must add at once, is in part based upon
the assumption--and how valid it is I simply do not know--
that educated Londoners would have been more powerfully
drawn to the theater than the illiterate or semi-illiterate
elements in Elizabethan society.

I believe that the Elizabethan who had a grammar s
school education behind him was probably better trained
to appreciate and understand a Shakespearean performance than the average adult spectator today. This opinion
I base not so much upon the substance of what was taught
as the way it was taught: the reading and listening habits
which were inculcated in the student at a time in his life
when they would have been likely to leave a permanent
impression upon him. From the time a boy entered grammar school, which was normally at the age of seven, to
the time he departed for trade or university, some seven
or eight years later, he was exposed to nothing but the
classical languages and literature, particularly the Latin
language and literature. It is almost unbelievable how
closely these boys were expected to read both prose and
poetry. John Brinsley was a practising schoolmaster
during the whole time Shakespeare was in London writing
his plays. In 1612 Brinsley published a book called Ludus
Literarius in which he expounds his teaching methods.
Here is how Brinsley would have his pupils approach the
study of the Latin poets.

In Virgil, Horace, and other the chiefe and most
approved Schoole Authors in poetry and prose,
to resolve any peece, for all these points of
learning and to do it in good Latine:

Construing, to give propriety of word and sense,
and also to expound in good phrase.

27

Scanning the Verses and giving a reason thereof.
Shewing the difficulties of Grammar.
Observing the Elegancies of Rhetoricke in Tropes
and Figures.
Noting Phrases and Epithets, with other principal
observations.

Brinsley advocates proceeding at the rate of about six or
eight verses a lesson. The object was clearly not to read
as much poetry as possible but to learn to read a little
of it well. I should add that, on several occasions, Brinsley assures the reader that his methods and aims differ,
where they differ at all, only in minor details from those
practised in the better grammar schools.

At the heart of the grammar school curriculum stood
the discipline of rhetoric. For the Renaissance, rhetoric
embraced the art of fine writing as well as the art of fine
speaking. It was a study of the manifold devices poets
and orators employed to depart from the normal, everyday patterns of language, "drawing it," in the words of th
the Elizabethan critic, Puttenham, "from plainesse and
simplicitie to a certain doubleness." These devices are
called Tropes and Figures. Many contemporary textbooks
of Rhetoric list as many as one hundred and fifty figures,
and the schoolboy was expected to know them all by heart,
together with their definitions, and to be able to identify
them whenever they appeared. He was also expected to
make a judicious use of them in composing his own Latin
verses in imitation of the classical poets. Renaissance
schoolmasters were cautious in this respect and almost
never permitted their charges "to meddle with making a
verse" (the phrase is Brinsley's) until they had reached
the ripe age of ten years old.

No age, I suppose, has produced a body of poetry
richer in brilliant and daring figures of speech than the
Renaissance. To what extent the Renaissance passion
for rhetoric contributed to this richness we can never
fully know. But one thing is certain. The poets of the
period and especially the dramatists would not have written in such a highly figurative manner unless they were

sure that they had in their audience many who were capable of responding to that type of writing. In this connection, I should like to quote the rhetorician Henry Peacham. He is speaking of synecdoche but his comment is obviously applicable to all figurative writing or speaking. "The Orator useth this figure chiefly when he is well persuaded concerning the wisdom of his hearers, that they are of sufficient capacity and understanding to collect his meaning, whereupon he maketh the bolder to remove his speech from the vulgar manner of speaking to figurative form whereby he giveth it a grace which otherwise it should want, forcing the understanding of his hearers to a deeper consideration of the sense and meaning."

It must be conceded, of course, that the Renaissance school system was idealistic in the extreme, and it is easy to find amusement in Brinsley's naive contention that, if other schoolmasters would follow his example, they would have their best pupils "in a short time attaine to that ripeness, that they who know not the places where they imitate, shall hardly discerne in many verses, whether the verses be Virgil's or the scholars." Schoolboys are schoolboys, and those of Elizabethan times could not have been greatly different from schoolboys today. But that is not precisely my point. My point is that the hard, driving methods of the Renaissance schoolmasters, their unflagging emphasis on the importance of the word and the phrase and the figure, and their faith in the technique of close imitation must inevitably have produced a body of readers and listeners whose response to poetry would be more than half-awake, who knew how to construe meaning, and who had been disciplined to make the effort. Let us not forget that neither Shakespeare himself nor his great contemporary, Ben Jonson, received more than a grammar school education.

Some years ago a book was published in this country with the challenging title, The Hamlet of Shakespeare's Audience. In this book, the author, a well-known scholar, by means of an historical reconstruction of the Elizabethan cultural environment, sought to prove, once and for all, how the audience must have responded to that play.

HARDING

"There is but one Hamlet, " he proclaims "and Shakespeare is its prophet, and all others are false. " His
guiding thesis is that the attitude which the Elizabethans
would have adopted toward the play would have been de-
cisively molded by their obsessive interest in politics
and statecraft. For them the theme of the play would
have been regicide. "The Renaissance feared anarchy, "
he reminds us, "and so detested even the idea of social
change. " Now in the play Claudius is king; he is also a
usurper and a murderer but he is still, for all that, ruling King of Denmark. He and his court therefore represent the status quo. Hamlet is the social rebel who threat-
ens the established order with wrack and ruin. Elizabethan sympathies would therefore have been with Claudius.
Infected as they were with the virus of Machiavellianism,
the moral issue would not have arisen to plague their
collective conscience. Instead, they would have admired
Claudius for his cleverness and skilled duplicity. And
this, writes the author of The Hamlet of Shakespeare's
Audience, is quite as it should be. "Whether one calls
Claudius good or bad depends... on one's ethical rigor-
ism...for like Iago, he follows the dictates of his position, age, and character. " Thus, the Elizabethans would
have taken the speeches of Claudius and the court party
at their face value. The author boldly accepts the inevi-
table consequences of this position. For example, we are
told that the Elizabethans would have taken Laertes' word
for it that Hamlet's love for Ophelia was "sweet, not
lasting. " What, then, becomes of Hamlet's protestations
of undying affection for Ophelia? What, indeed, becomes
of Hamlet? A prince of shreds and patches, whose "simple, military standards of life" leave him defenceless
against the "practical statesmanship" of Polonius. If at
times it appears that, in the exchanges of witty banter,
Hamlet emerges the winner, this is only because Polonius and others concede to him "the royal privilege of
getting the best of all the repartee. "

Something is painfully wrong here. And the wrong-
ness, I am convinced, lies not in the method but the application. It is the application which is faulty. Books

30

like the one I have just mentioned can be extremely useful in restoring to the plays of Shakespeare meanings
which the passing years have obscured or in some case
obliterated. And even where such books cannot truly be
said to perform so positive a function, they may still
have the negative virtue of imposing healthy restraints
upon our freedom of interpretation. But there is no virtue in the indiscriminate importation of ideas from the
world outside the play to elucidate its meanings. I do not
doubt that there were individuals in Shakespeare's audience who were morally so constituted that they were able
to give Claudius their unqualified admiration. There are
Machiavellians in every audience, audiences then and
audiences now. But to argue that the morality of Claudius
would not have been an issue with the audience is, simply
and egregiously, to ignore the play. Claudius is guilt-
ridden; the play says so and not once but many times,
explicitly and implicitly, and, in such matters the play
is not to be denied. Here we have an open-and-shut case;
the idea imported from the world outside the play is in
open collision with the words of the play.

Should we then wholly abandon the idea? I think not.
Provided that we guard against too rigorous an application, the idea ought to prove a valuable adjunct in helping
us to understand the play. For the Elizabethans unques-
tionably did hate and fear the idea of social change. It
does not follow from this, however, that they would have
forgiven Claudius the sins for which he could not forgive
himself. What does follow, I believe, is that the Elizabethans would have been much more sensitive than we
are, and perhaps can be, to the nature of Hamlet's tragic
dilemma--Hamlet, whose humanity has been so brilliant-
ly defined for us that we are prone to forget, as Mr. T. S.
Eliot seems to have once forgotten, that Hamlet is also
Prince of Denmark. He is not himself alone.

We must therefore, in the first place, be very careful about the assumptions and preoccupations which we
ascribe to Shakespeare's audience as a totality. No audience, except the Greek audience, has been so heterogeneous in its composition, with people from all stations of

31

life, from the lowest to the highest, from the poorest to
the richest, from the uneducated to the highly educated.
And secondly, we should be especially careful in the application of these assumptions, remembering that the
plays of Shakespeare are designed primarily to produce
certain emotional and imaginative effects, <u>in the theater
itself,</u> and that these effects may be sufficiently powerful
to override or qualify, or alter in some way, the most
deep-seated of assumptions.

Above all, we must not let Shakespeare's audience
get the better of us. It is the plays which have survived
and not the people for which they were written. There
are many useful things to be learned from the contemporary audience but we must keep it in its honored place.
We are grateful to that audience of course. Its popular,
universal character must have served as a constant challenge to Shakespeare to probe below all the surface differences to the timeless, human qualities which make
us know, for better or for worse, something of what it
is to be a man. We simply cannot afford, at this late date,
to give Shakespeare back to the Elizabethans--even assuming that we could.

Helge Kökeritz

SHAKESPEARE'S LANGUAGE

"To gaine the Language,
'Tis needfull, that the most
immodest word
Be look'd upon, and learn'd. "

--2 Henry IV (4. 4. 69-71)

February 10, 1954

Some time ago the mail brought me a book catalog
entitled "An Unusual Collection in Drama, Cinema,
Theatre. " Since it included a special section on Shakespeare, I did not throw it into the wastepaper basket at
once. Instead I began to scan its odd assortment of some
400 titles of Shakespeareana. Here is a handful of them,
without their authors' names: Aspects of Shakespeare;
The Shakespeare Symphony; Shakespeare's Imagination;
Shakespeare and Home Life; Shakespeare and Science;
The Birds of Shakespeare; The Shakespeare Flora;
Shakespeare at Work; Sergeant Shakespeare; Shake-
speare Identified; Shakespeare Rediscovered; Seven
Shakespeares. A dozen titles out of 400, a fair sampling,
I would say, of what is sometimes referred to as "the
Shakespeare industry" or "Shakespeare idolatry". More
often than not these two terms appear to be synonymous.
Even if the catalog did not list a recently published vol-
ume with sensational disclosures about the elusive figure
named William Shakespeare, it offered for sale other
Shakespeare fiction stories, e. g. Bacon in Shakespeare
and Lord Oxford was Shakespeare. To be sure, these
represent the negative side of the same Shakespeare
idolatry and need not, therefore, disturb us at all. For
every religion, including the cult of Shakespeare, is
bound to have its dissenters and apostates, who will be
a thorn in the flesh of all true believers.

What, in my opinion, is far more disturbing than
these recurring identifications of Shakespeare with somebody else, is the increasing preoccupation today with
Shakespearean trivia. Our learned journals are all too
willing to provide space for articles which, despite an

impressive jargon, often manage to say nothing or next to nothing. Equally disturbing to me is the modern trend to allegorize Shakespeare in the manner of the medieval Schoolmen, that is, to use his plays, as it were, like medieval exempla to be expounded into more or less subtle homilies for the spiritual welfare of the Shakespeare reader. Be that as it may, sooner or later scholars and students will discover that many an alluring avenue to Shakespeare actually leads into a cul-de-sac. And then they may turn to the study of his language as a means of revitalizing what is already threatening to become sterile and unprofitable. If they have the right qualifications for philological inquiry and the right attitude to it, they are bound to prosper.

It is odd, somehow, that the study of Shakespeare's language has not been able to keep pace with the study of his plays as dramatic compositions. One would have thought that his language, the obvious medium of his art, would command at least as much interest as his sources, his dramatic technique, his philosophy, and so forth. This is not so, however. I think it is symptomatic of this indifference to Shakespeare's language that of the 400 titles just mentioned only nine dealt with certain aspects of it. That is to say, approximately 2 percent, a figure which is probably far too high if everything written about Shakespeare were considered. Apart from Abbott's somewhat antiquated Shakespearian Grammar of 1870, Schmidt's Shakespeare-Lexicon, and Cunliffe's Shakespeare Glossary, the remaining six volumes are of no value whatever today. Let me quote one title only to convince you that my verdict is anything but ungenerous. In 1887 Charles Mackay published in London A Glossary of Obscure Words and Phrases in the Writings of Shakespeare and His Contemporaries, Traced Etymologically to the Ancient Language of the British People as spoken before the Irruption of the Danes and Saxons. Yet this fanciful product of Celtomania is characterized in the Catalog as "very important and scarce." It may be scarce, but scarcity is certainly not a criterion of importance, at least not in this particular case.

SHAKESPEARE'S LANGUAGE

In 1928 the late Professor George Gordon of Oxford summed up the situation as follows in his stimulating paper "Shakespeare's English" (S. P. E. Tract No. XXIX, p. 265): "A book on Shakespeare's language, considered in its whole extent, is badly wanted. I have waited so long for some one else to write it that I have decided to wait no longer, and, incited by Mr. Onions, am now writing it myself." Unfortunately Professor Gordon never lived to complete the book, and I doubt that his manuscript notes have been preserved. Indeed, like Professor Gordon we are probably all waiting for some one else to write such a book--or perhaps I should say, we are waiting for some one else to begin the thorough analyses of various aspects of Shakespeare's language on which it will eventually be possible to base a comprehensive survey of his language as a whole. The subject is so vast, so diversified, and so little has actually been done in the field that it would be sheer presumption at this stage if anyone tried to characterize Shakespeare's language in other than the most general terms. Rather than perpetrating such generalities, rather than trying to draw an impressionistic portrait of Shakespeare the Linguistic Master-builder--something I probably could not do anyhow--I shall devote the rest of this lecture to a brief summary of what has so far been achieved in the field and to a rapid sketch of all that remains to be done. Here and there I may be able to inject some original observations on minor problems which seem capable of solution without the need of a considerable body of comparative material.

Though it is true to say that Shakespeare's language in general has been sadly neglected by scholars, we possess nevertheless some basic investigations which will provide the student of Shakespeare and other Renaissance writers with useful tools. Thus we have a Shakespeare-Lexicon, first published in 1874 by Alexander Schmidt and revised after his death by Gregor Sarrazin in 1901; it was last reprinted in 1923. Though it could well stand another thorough revision, it is nevertheless a remarkably competent piece of work. C. T. Onions'

Shakespeare Glossary, first published in 1911 and since
then revised and reprinted several times, is much more
compact than Schmidt's Lexicon but no less significant,
as may be expected from one of the principal editors of
the Oxford English Dictionary. This is practically all
we have in the way of comprehensive Shakespearean
word-studies, except, of course, for the glosses and
notes in modern editions of his plays and poems.

Usually the glossing is done very judiciously, but
at times it is apt to be conjectural or fanciful. Take for
instance G. B. Harrison's interpretation of tie as 'trim
short' in Measure for Measure 4. 2. 187: "Shave the head
and tie the beard." No such meaning of tie is on record,
and unless Harrison can prove, by quoting chapter and
verse, that the verb tie could mean 'to trim', it is irresponsible to gloss it in that way. Either tie must be in-
terpreted 'to bind up' or tie is a misprint in the Folio;
some editors think so and emend it to dye, a highly
plausible suggestion considering the explicit reference
to the color of Claudio's beard in the next scene ("A man
of Claudio's years, his beard and head / Just of his
color" - 4. 3. 76 f.). Emendation should, however, be
avoided at all cost, unless it can make sense out of an
otherwise meaningless passage. In this particular case,
tie 'to bind up' does make sense, though admittedly the
reason why the culprit's beard should be 'bound up' (or
'trimmed') before execution is none too apparent. To
my knowledge no one ever had his head chopped off face
upward, so why bother to tie up or trim the poor devil's
beard? The logic of the plot requires a word like dye,
but the text has tie, thus leaving the conscientious modern editor caught on the horns of a dilemma. I have
adduced this example to illustrate the extreme care an
editor must exercise in glossing and annotating Shakespeare. As a rule the splendid Oxford English Dictionary seldom lets him down, but at times it may be advisable for him to consult such contemporary dictionaries
as Florio's A Worlde of Words (1598) and Cotgrave's
A Dictionarie of the French and English Tonges (1611).
I am glad to say that the editors of the new Yale

SHAKESPEARE'S LANGUAGE

Shakespeare are aware of these useful sources of 16th-
and 17th- century wordlore.

Besides these dictionaries and glossaries we are fortunate in having a fine Shakespearean Grammar by Wil-
helm Franz, which has superseded Abbott's of 1870.
Franz's Shakespeare-Grammatik, which first appeared
in 1899, has been kept up-to-date by several revisions,
the latest in 1939, shortly before its author's death. The
1939 edition bears the curious title, Die Sprache Shakespeares in Vers und Prosa unter Berücksichtigung des
Amerikanischen entwicklungsgeschichtlich dargestellt.
(The Language of Shakespeare in Verse and Prose treated
historically and with due reference to American English).
First of all, Franz does not give a comprehensive account
of Shakespeare's language as the title would seem to indicate. The main part of the book, about 450 pages, is
devoted to a careful, reliable analysis of Shakespeare's
grammar and syntax; in many respects this sets a model
for similar investigations that will attempt nothing beyond
a strict record of grammatical and syntactical phenomena.
The remaining 250 pages include a brief but useful survey
of Shakespearean word-formation, a Shakespearean prosody in outline, a most unsatisfactory sketch of Shakespeare's pronunciation, two or three other essays, and
finally a superficial comparison of British and American
English comprising ten pages in all.

It is difficult to understand why Franz wanted to in-
corporate this section on American English. Even if he
was anxious to stress certain similarities between
Shakespeare's language and the language that came to
this country in 1620 and later, it was foolish of him to
attempt such a comparison here, because his material
was by no means adequate for a treatment of this kind,
nor was a Shakespearean Grammar the right place for it.
Anyhow, Franz's thorough analysis of Shakespeare's
grammar and syntax does not preclude further work in
the field. We need, for instance, to compare Shakespeare's usage with that of his predecessors, his contemporaries and his immediate successors so as to be
able to single out possible idiosyncrasies of his and relate

him more definitely to the conservative and progressive trends in the language of his day. Moreover, it may even be worth while studying the syntax of some of his dramatis personae, especially if this were done in connection with a stylistic analysis of their speeches.

One phase of Shakespeare's language that has at last been adequately surveyed--if I am permitted to say so myself--is his pronunciation. I am convinced that there is little likelihood of any major phonological discoveries in the future that would seriously affect the sound-system as reconstructed in my recently published Shakespeare's Pronunciation. On the other hand, future research in 15th-, 16th-, and 17th-century phonology may well make it possible to determine more precisely the pronunciation of individual words which at present seem to allow of more than one phonological interpretation. Indeed, many obscure points still remain to be solved, and it is to be hoped that those interested in historical phonology will continue my work by investigating the pronunciation of other Renaissance writers in a similar fashion.

This all but exhausts the list of significant contributions to the study of Shakespeare's language. To be sure, quite a few articles have appeared in the last fifty or a hundred years dealing with linguistic details of one sort or another in Shakespeare's works, but only a few of them are of any real significance; this is true particularly of Professor Gordon's paper quoted above, Gladys Doidge Willcock's "Shakespeare as Critic of Language, " and F. P. Wilson's "Shakespeare and the Diction of Common Life, " which clearly show what could rewardingly be done on a much larger scale.

It is a commonplace nowadays to emphasize Shakespeare's verbal ingenuity, to represent him as a language maker, a man who enriched the English language with words and phrases of every conceivable type, from the coarsest rusticisms and slang to the most recondite inkhorn terms. In like manner Chaucer was once hailed as the father of the English language. That romantic notion has now fortunately been abandoned, and it is, indeed,

high time that we come down to earth also when trying
to evaluate Shakespeare's linguistic genius. It will not
detract one jot from his greatness if instead of treating
him as a demigod we attempt, soberly and realistically,
to relate him to the linguistic currents of the closing 16th
century. For after all, Shakespeare was a human being,
a vigorous, warmblooded, sensitive Elizabethan among
Elizabethans. He saw what they saw, heard what they
heard, spoke as they did, thought their thoughts and expressed them in the manner of the day. However, since
he was by nature a poet and by profession an actor-play-
wright, he often did it far better than most of his contemporaries. But because he was human, he inevitably
blundered now and then. His mind must have been amaz-
ingly receptive. Like a sponge it sucked up everything
he heard or read and stored it away for future use. And
when he took goosequill in hand, ideas and words came
tumbling out at breakneck speed, or as Heminge and
Condell describe it in their Preface to the First Folio,
"His mind and hand went together: And what he thought,
he uttered with that easinesse, that wee have scarce received from him a blot in his papers." What he thought
and uttered was exuberantly Elizabethan, both in substance and form.

I agree with Professor Gordon when he characterizes the language of the period in this way (p. 259): "The
first quality of Elizabethan, and therefore of Shakespearian English, is its power of hospitality, its passion
of free experiment, its willingness to use every form of
verbal wealth, to try anything." But I cannot help feeling that Gordon is becoming much too romantic when he
goes on to say about Shakespeare (pp. 264 f.): "He was,
by every sign--indeed the evidence is overwhelming--in
the first rank of the advance, and of all its members the
most exuberant; an experimenter always, though in the
diction of his time; making his language as he went along.
Only the Americans to-day profess to do this." There
is an element of truth in the comparison of the Elizabethan attitude to the English language and that of present-day Americans. The Elizabethans were, however,

41

much less hampered by any ideas of correctness. They said, and Shakespeare said, "It is me," "Between you and I, " etc., something not many self-respecting Americans would dare to do today in print. My own investigations of Shakespeare's pronunciation have revealed that it differed in no way from what was then good colloquial usage. And this is equally true of his grammar and syntax.

It was for the 18th century, the age of reason and correctness, to draw up many of the grammatical rules which now bother most of us. Shakespeare never cared whether it was correct or incorrect to say he is rode, he is rid, or he is ridden--he used all three as it suited his fancy, the euphony of the line and its meter. And so did everybody else in his day. I cannot imagine that he hesitated for a moment whether to use be, are, or is for the modern plural are. Thus in The Merry Wives of Windsor (1.1.98-99) Slender asks: "Be there Beares ith' Towne?" to which Anne answers: "I thinke there are, Sir, " while in Twelfth Night (3.2.84-85) Maria says: "More lynes then is in the new Mappe. " Such variation bears testimony to free and easy composition. Juliet's words (3.2.127), "Where is my Father and my Mother Nurse?" reproduces exactly the natural syntax of spoken English, and so do numerous parallel cases from other Shakespearean plays.

Now, if this colloquiality is typical of Shakespeare's pronunciation, grammar, and syntax, why should it not manifest itself equally well in his vocabulary? Or to state the question differently, why should he necessarily have created a host of new words or derivatives instead of simply using what was already available? It may be objected, of course, that the vocabulary allows of greater freedom at the hand of an articulate writer, that, indeed, word-formation and word-manipulation are the privilege and hallmark of the genius. That may be so-- but how do we know that Shakespeare really created or was even the first user of the words or connotations with which he is generally credited? Our statistics are based almost exclusively on the Oxford English Diction-

ary, which has registered very carefully the language of
Shakespeare and his contemporaries, but has omitted to
excerpt much other relevant material of one sort or another. So, if a certain word or connotation is recorded in
the Oxford English Dictionary only from Shakespeare, or
his use of either is the first instance cited, what does
that prove? Nothing beyond the fact that Shakespeare did
use the particular word or connotation.

We have no contemporary record of the spoken language of the day, what people talked of and how they said
it, nor do we possess anything like complete data from
either printed or unprinted sources--the quotations in the
Oxford English Dictionary represent only selective reading. Anyone who works with unprinted documents will
nearly always be able to antedate the Oxford English Dictionary, sometimes by as much as 200 years. I am sure
that if we could excerpt everything written during the Renaissance, we might remove most, perhaps all, of the
words now listed as exclusively Shakespearean. It is
surprising that Gordon, who warned his readers against
placing too much reliance on the Oxford English Dictionary in this respect, nevertheless lists about 70 words as
either coined by or introduced by Shakespeare. On the
other hand the great George Lyman Kittredge of Harvard
sometimes went to the other extreme: he refused to believe in a pun to't - toot in Othello 3.1.16: 'If you have
any Musicke that may not be heard, too't againe. " His
argument for rejecting this pun was that toot itself did
not occur in Shakespeare! Yet toot is recorded from
1510 in the Oxford English Dictionary and was obviously
then an onomatopoetic word of long standing in the language. Toot is simply one of many hidden words in
Shakespeare--I call them 'hidden' because they have
come to light only through a careful study of his homo-
nymic puns. Other such words which I can claim to have
restored to Shakespeare's vocabulary are, e.g., bile,
cleam, departer, fay 'to cleanse', fise 'to break wind',
foin 'fur', harden 'a coarse fabric of flax' (used in a pun
on Arden), heal 'health', knob 'pimple', nick 'slit',
quoin, ray 'to soil', rime, rung 'cudgel', seisin, tear

'of good quality' (used in a pun on the verb tear in the
name of Doll Tearsheet), thief (or theave) 'young ewe',
not to mention several Elizabethan household words which
might offend the ears of the present audience, were I to
utter them here, though one of them at least is a term
of high frequency in From Here to Eternity. When sooner or later some dauntless scholar embarks on an exhaustive study of Shakespeare's semantic puns--a gigan-
tic undertaking but well worth the effort--then I am sure
we shall be able to add as well a sizeable number of hidden connotations to those already recorded.

Shakespearean word-studies should not, however,
limit themselves to establishing the scope and prove-
nance of his vocabulary and to defining the meanings and
connotations of each vocable. Of interest would be an
investigation into the words Shakespeare did not use himself but which occur more or less frequently in his predecessors and contemporaries. This might unearth material of importance in solving problems of authorship,
textual transmission and the like. Of greater importance
would be an inquiry into the stylistic usage of native
words versus learned borrowings, above all as a means
of characterization.

Shakespeare himself was word-conscious, and so
were the characters he created, like their Elizabethan
prototypes. Even his lowest characters betray the same
interest in words. Some of them, e.g. Dogberry and
Mrs. Quickly, do so by misusing the learned words of
their superiors--we call this tendency, somewhat anach-
ronistically, malapropism. Others have become so in-
fatuated with the modish terms that they must use them
on every conceivable occasion; thus Nym in The Merry
Wives of Windsor can hardly utter a sentence without
putting in the word humor: "I like not the humor of lying:
hee hath wronged me in some humors: I should have
borne the humour'd Letter to her" (2.1.132-135). Pistol
in the same play pretends to be shocked by Nym's forth-
right steal and reprimands him: "Convay: the wise it call:
Steale? foh: a fico for the phrase" (1.3.32-33), while
Doll Tearsheet appears to be disgusted with the degrada-

tion that the word occupy has suffered in common par-
lance: "God's light, these villaines wil make the word
as odious as the word occupy, which was an excellent
good worde before it was il sorted" (2 Henry IV 2.4.160-
162) - cf. Ben Jonson's dictum, "Many, out of their ob-
scene Apprehensions, refuse proper and fit words; as
occupie, nature, and the like" (Oxford English Dictionary). Hamlet parodies Osric's affected lingo so adroitly
that the latter is almost nonplussed. And one whole play,
Love's Labor's Lost, is--as Miss Wilcock has stressed
--"a great game of language played with unfailing verve
from the first act to the last." Yet, no one has so far
made an exhaustive study of it from that point of view,
nor has, for that matter, anyone investigated the language of satire and parody as used by Shakespeare. But
Arthur King has done so in respect of Ben Jonson's language in his model socio-stylistic study The Language
of Satirized Characters in Poëtaster.

The Elizabethans were great and unblushing imita-
tors. Everybody imitated somebody else. As King has
observed (pp. xix ff.), scholars imitated the ancients
into the vernacular and the upper classes imitated foreigners and scholars; the lower classes imitated the upper classes. "In the former stage of imitation the fashion is formed, in the latter it moves down the community."
Contact with foreigners, through travel, commerce, and
reading, introduced in England styles and manners of behavior and language. Similarly the preoccupation of
scholars with classical literature and language gave rise
to the understandable but none the less absurd notion
that the English language was not copious enough for literary use. It had to be enriched, and it was enriched by
the wholesale importation or adoption of Latin and Greek
words and phrases. This was the second wave of loan-
flux that interfered with the natural growth of the lan-
guage--the first one occurred in Middle English times,
particularly in the 13th and 14th centuries, when thousands of French words were adopted. Those who thought
and wrote in Latin were usually disinclined, or simply
too lazy, to utilize the natural resources of the language,

that is to say, to find native words for the abstract terms they were familiar with in Latin or Greek. Instead they merely employed the foreign words in speaking or writing English, ignoring all those who had only "small Latin and less Greek", or none at all. When such neologisms were imitated by those who did not know the languages from which they had been culled, the result was bound to be semantic vagueness. Thus the coexistence of ingenious (from French ingénieux, talented) and ingenuous (from Latin ingenuus, native) caused confusion between the two: Shakespeare uses ingenuous for ingenious three times (Love's Labor's Lost 1.2.29, 4.2.80, Cymbeline 4.2.186), unless they are all misprints; this seems to be the case in Love's Labor's Lost 4.2.80, where the Folio has ingennous and the Quarto ingenous. Today we have ingenuity, which originally meant 'ingenuousness', as the noun of ingenious--if we were correct we should say instead ingeniosity. Such semantic muddles are not uncommon in Shakespeare, but their occurrence is often taken as evidence of his creative and acquisitive power.

Let me illustrate this point with a small group of words which reflect the confusion of like-sounding and semantically related words. In his valuable introduction to Gordon's Nine Plays of Shakespeare, Onions makes much of Shakespeare's use of the suffixes -able and -ible as in deceivable, defensible, without, however, getting to the core of the problem. Defensible, which now means only 'that can be defended', has in Shakespeare the sense 'capable of making a defense, defensive', as in Henry V 3.3.50, where the Governor of Harfleur tells the King: "Enter our Gates, dispose of us and ours, / For we no longer are defensible"--that is, 'capable of defending ourselves'. According to the Oxford English Dictionary this is the original meaning of the adjective, first recorded in 1297 in the form defensable and later remodeled to defensible on the pattern of Latin defensibilem. The meaning 'capable of making a defense' is not far removed from that of defensive (from French défensif) 'having the quality of defending against injury, serving as defense, protective', as in Richard II 2.1.48, where old Gaunt speaks of the sea surrounding England "as a Moate defensive to a house. " This confusion of _defensive_ and _defensible_ can be evidenced even from Ben Jonson and Milton despite their superior Latin background (see quotations in the _Oxford English Dictionary_). Similarly _plausive_ and _plausible_ get mixed up; _plausive_ meant 'expressive of approval by applause' as in Heywood's phrase "those plausive shouts", but _plausible_ meant 'deserving of applause, laudable, commendable', as in _Measure_ for _Measure_ 3.1.253: "With a plausible obedience"; this sense is first recorded in 1561. But in _Hamlet_ 1.4.30 Hamlet criticizes "some habit, that too much ore-leavens / The forme of plausive manners, " that is 'laudable, pleasing manners'. This also happens in _All's Well_ 1.2.51, where we find "his plausive words"--in both cases _plausive_ fits the scansion better than _plausible_ would have done. Indeed, there is much to suggest that _plausive_ and _plausible_ were rhythmical variants in Shakespeare's language.

That the rhythm of the line prompted the use of one or the other of two synonyms can be convincingly demonstrated in the case of _deceivable_ and _deceitful_; in _Twelfth Night_ 4.3.21 Sebastian exclaims: "There's something in't / That is deceivable, " where _deceivable_ means 'deceitful' (a meaning recorded from 1303). But _deceitful_ itself always appears where a trisyllabic word is needed, e. g. "Is this thy cunning, thou deceitfull Dame?" (_1 Henry VI_ 2.1.50). The semantic vagueness of many words ending in _-ive_ and _-ible_ may have been furthered by phonetic causes: the like-sounding _plausive_ and _plausible_, _defensive_ and _defensible_ become almost indistinguishable when the adverbial ending _-ly_ is added: _plausively - plausibly_, _defensively - defensibly_. Note particularly _The Rape of Lucrece_ 1854: "The Romans plausibly did give consent, " where _plausibly_ means 'with applause, approvingly', that is, 'plausively'. It may be added here that in 1581 Mulcaster, Headmaster of St. Paul's School and a classical scholar, wrote _plausibly_ when he meant _plausively_: "His judgment is so often, and so plausibly vouched by the curteouse maister Askam" (_Oxford English Dictionary_).

Anyhow, it is important to remember that in Shakespeare and other contemporary poets doublets like
plausive and plausible must have been regarded as met-
rically useful variants; in other words, if the poet needed a disyllabic word he wrote plausive, if a trisyllabic
one plausible. That is the simple reason why both Shakespeare and Milton used unexpressive and not unexpress-
able or inexpressible, Shakespeare in Orlando's spirited
couplet (As You Like It 3.2.10-11): "Run, run Orlando,
carve on every Tree, / The faire, the chaste, and unexpressive shee, " and Milton more solemnly in the Hymn
on the Morning of Christ's Nativity (11): "Harping in
loud and solemn quire, / With unexpressive notes to
Heav'n's new-born Heir" (note by the way the interesting
rhyme, with quire pronounced 'quair'). The scansion of
the line doubtless prompted the use of insuppressive in
Julius Caesar 2.1.134: "Nor th'insuppressive Mettle of
our Spirits"; the variant insuppressible, not found in
Shakespeare, is recorded from 1620. In the same way
we must explain the nonce-formation directive 'able to
be directed' in Troilus and Cressida 1.3.356-57: "Swords
and Bowes / Directive by the Limbes"; here directive,
which should have been directible or directable (only the
latter is on record, from the 19th century), may be a
genuine Shakespearean formation on the analogy of other
words with interchangeable -ive and -ible.

This correlation of word-form and prosody can be
seen very clearly in Shakespeare's use of such doublets
as pale and paly, vast and vasty. Paly and vasty appear
only where two syllables are required, e. g. in Henry V
4.pr.8: "And through their paly flames / Each Battaile
sees the others umber'd face, " and from the same play
(the prologue to Act 1): "Can this Cock-Pit hold / The
vastie fields of France?" Extended, analogical forms
like these, which are in a sense double adjectives, since
they consist of a simple, usually monosyllabic, adjective
plus the extra adjectival suffix -y, are on record from
1400 but are doubtless much older. Hugey and leany are
among the earliest; Spenser, for instance, has leany in
The Shepherd's Calendar (July 199): "They han fatte

kernes, and leany knaves. " These double adjectives must
have been colloquial formations on the pattern of icy,
happy, dirty, etc. , which were far more frequent than
the monosyllabic cool, lean, pale, etc. Mrs. Quickly's
jealousy for jealous ("hee's a very jealousie-man"
Merry Wives 2.2.93) is a derivative of the same kind or
a very natural misuse of the noun as an adjective in -y;
Shakespeare had no doubt often heard jealousy used col-
loquially or vulgarly in that way and with his keen sense
of linguistic realism he placed it in the mouth of blunder-
lingly word-conscious Mrs. Quickly. I suspect that the
increasing popularity of adjectives like paly, leany, etc. ,
in the 16th and 17th centuries is due to no other factor
than that the poets found them most convenient as prosodic variants of pale, lean, etc. ; from the poets they auto-
matically found their way into the Oxford English Dictionary. In Queen Elizabeth's "Englishing" of Boethius' De
Consolatione Philosophiae we come across greeny, spelled
griny, twice, in Carew and Spenser cooly ("the cooly
shade"), and so on. It was therefore quite natural for
the artisan-playwright in A Midsummer Night's Dream
to call Pyramus "Most brisky Juvenall, and eke most
lovely Jew. " (3.1.97), and for the drinking-song in Antony
and Cleopatra (2.7.119) to have "Plumpie Bacchus, with
pinke eyne. " Even though brisky may have sounded
slightly jocular in connection with Juvenall, both brisky
and plumpy were strictly within the prosodic and rhetorical tradition of the day.

It is, indeed, a grave misunderstanding of Shakespeare's language when Gordon characterizes (p. 274)
Shakespeare's starry, testy, batty, wormy in A Midsummer Night's Dream (3.2.356-84) as "drops in that
delicate rain of nicely calculated rusticity with which
Shakespeare has sprinkled the language of this play. "
First of all, testy is a French word with no rustic flavor whatsoever; it comes from testif and is consequently not a derivative in -y like the others. Secondly,
starry welkin, which Gordon takes to be a strange mis-
alliance between this rustic starry and "the archaic and
ludicrous welkin" was a contemporary cliché, a variant

of <u>starry heaven,</u> <u>starry sphere,</u> <u>starry sky,</u> <u>starry</u>
<u>cope,</u> <u>starry canopy,</u> etc. <u>Starry</u> itself was certainly
not a rustic word, nor was <u>welkin</u> archaic and ludicrous
in the 16th century; Shakespeare uses <u>welkin</u> twice in
his poems and seventeen times in his plays--it was
probably literary rather than colloquial, though it has
survived down to this day in some northern dialects. A
cliché of the same kind as <u>starry welkin</u> is <u>wormy bed,</u>
which even Milton did not hesitate to employ in <u>The</u>
<u>Death of a Fair Infant</u>: "Yet can I not persuade me thou
art dead . . . Or that thy beauties lie in wormy bed. "
Whatever its esoteric quality, the passage from <u>A Mid-</u>
<u>summer Night's Dream</u> to which Gordon refers, was
definitely neither rustic nor archaic.

So much for Shakespeare's vocabulary. I am afraid
I have spent too much time on it and shall therefore have
to touch only in passing on two aspects of Shakespeare's
language which need to be investigated by competent
philologists. One is Shakespeare's style, the other is
his prosody. Of course, everybody talks very glibly
about Shakespeare's early style, about his mature style,
and so forth, but to my knowledge no one has as yet attempted a strict philological analysis of either; the rhetorical background, however, has been dealt with fairly
satisfactorily by Sister Miriam Joseph in <u>Shakespeare's</u>
<u>Use of the Arts of Language</u>, though her lack of philo-
logical training is a serious weakness. The situation is
much worse when we come to Shakespeare's prosody.
To be sure, there is no lack of prosodic studies of Shakespeare, but the supposedly authoritative ones have all
been undertaken by amateurs with not even a rudimentary
knowledge of 16th-century phonology. Is it surprising
then that the strangest ideas prevail today concerning
the principles of Shakespeare's versification?

For almost an hour I have taken you on a philolo-
gist's tedious rambles along the fringes of the only par-
tially explored territory of Shakespeare's language.
Once or twice we have made short reconnoitering ex-

peditions into the interior and have returned with data
that invite more extensive exploration. Indeed, here
lies the frontier of Shakespearean scholarship. For
generations it has been waiting for the hardy pioneer to
come and stake out his claim. Here are vast areas of
virgin soil, which promise rich harvests to anyone who
is prepared to dig and ditch, to lay out roads and bridge
streams, to blast the rock and clear the underbrush.
But one cannot just walk into the wilderness unprepared
--one must take along some essential equipment in order
to succeed, the indispensable tools of philological exploration. And one must have enthusiasm for the drudg-
ery ahead, an ardent desire to know as much as possible
of this fruitful territory, the English language of the
Renaissance, which is also Shakespeare's language.

Frank McMullan

PRODUCING SHAKESPEARE

> Thus with imagined wing our
>   swift scene flies
> In motion of no less celerity
> Than that of thought.
>
>   --<u>King Henry V</u>
>   (3. Prologue.1-3)

February 15, 1954

This series of lectures, the exhibits of Elizabethan manuscripts, and the production of The Merry Wives of Windsor included in the Shakespeare Festival at Yale symbolize the present-day collaboration between scholarship and the theatre. This collaboration is taken for granted now. It is easy to forget that many scholars back in the 19th century agreed wholeheartedly when Charles Lamb, in 1811, wrote in The Reflector: "I cannot help being of the opinion that the plays of Shakespeare are less calculated for performance on a stage, than those of almost any other dramatist whatever."

Theatrical scholarship has markedly affected the critical interpretations of the plays since this pronouncement. Beginning with George Pierce Baker's The Development of Shakespeare as a Dramatist in 1907, when he tried to analyze the plays "not as character studies or as philosophic disquisitions, but as pieces written by a practical actor-author aiming at immediate popular success," and Brander Matthews' similarly conceived book Shakespeare as a Playwright, we come today to J. Dover Wilson's belief that Shakespeare wrote "not books but promptbooks, or, if you will, theatrical scores for the performance of moving pageants of speech, action, and colour, upon a particular stage by a particular troupe of actors for a particular audience." (Allardyce Nicoll in Shakespeare Survey, (Cambridge, Cambridge University Press, 1948, p. 13.)

The contribution I hope to make to this series of lectures, devoted to a greater understanding of Shakespeare, is in terms of this fundamental concept. My findings are based upon the history of Shakespeare on the stage and

practical experience gained from working with the plays
of Shakespeare through the media of actors and the physical elements of production. The modern producer of
Shakespeare must be concerned primarily with footlights,
though continually aware of footnotes. Therefore it is to
the theatre that the director must go. However, he will
be wise if he rummages through the warehouse of theatrical history--where footlights illuminate footnotes--
before facing the actual task of producing Shakespeare.
I propose, then, to look back on the past to see Shakespeare on the stage, to find the theories and practices
which can enlighten the modern director.

In the 1949 issue of Shakespeare Survey Miss Muriel
St. Clare Byrne, writing on "Fifty Years of Shakespearian
Production: 1898-1948, "makes an excellent guide in
pointing out the landmarks, influences, and traditions.
Instead of starting with these dates, however, she says
(p. 1) that "To understand the methods and achievements
of Shakespearian production in the first half of this century we must turn to the last 50 years of the nineteenth. "
We learn that the English theatre of that era made an important discovery: It found that the plays of Shakespeare
demand special consideration. The great actor-manager
of the day, John Philip Kemble, and later his brother
Charles, realizing this fact, introduced specially designed scenery for Shakespeare. Charles' much praised
spectacular production of King John in 1824 set a prece-
dent for settings based upon archeology and social history, and established itself as a dominant consideration.
Costume had to be correct for plays which could be assigned to definite historical epochs and countries. It is
interesting to stop a moment and recall that Stanislavsky,
writing in My Life in Art, (Boston, Little, Brown, 1935)
describes the extensive preparations for the Moscow Art
Theatre's production of Julius Caesar in 1904 which were
based entirely on the same principles motivating the
Kembles. He says (pp. 408, 409, 412, 414) that
Nemirovich-Danchenko, his co-director of the Moscow
Art Theatre, and the designer Simov went to Rome to
gather material,

and a regular office was established in the
theatre to take care of the preparatory work.
. . . We established a series of departments.
. . . One of the departments took care of the
literary side of the play, and its texts, its
changes and cuts, its translation, its comparison with other texts of the same play,
and researches in foreign and domestic publications, criticism and so on. Another department took care of all that treated of the
locale, the social conditions of life, the cus-
toms, buildings, and usages of the time of
Caesar.

He goes on to describe the great pains they took to dupli-
cate a Roman street in the time of Caesar.

Rows of stores stretched from the forestage
into the trap and were lost in the movement
of the crowd. Merchants stood in front of
them, calling the buyers; here and there was
seen the shop of an armorer where the swords,
shields and armor were in the process of forg-
ing, and in the necessary places the ringing of
the hammers in the shop covered the talk of
the crowd. The street passed along the whole
width of the stage and disappeared in the wings,
while on the right an alley with a typical Italian
stairway poured into it from the hills. In this
way the citizens moved towards each other, up
and down and along the stage, and their move-
ments on meeting created a garish and lifelike
picture of Roman street life. . . . In the intimate life of the theatre there was created a
cross-section of antique social life . . .

I make reference to this excerpt from theatrical history
to emphasize the fact that as late as the first years of
the 20th century historical accuracy, naturalism, and

spectacle underlay a philosophy of Shakespearean production conceived originally by the Kembles in the first decades of the 19th century. ". . . the appeal of spectacle
(in the 19th century) was so much stronger than that of the
full text that Macready was moved to describe Edmund
Kean's productions as scenes annotated by the texts. . . .
Kean's spectacles determined the main trend in English
Shakespearean production for 60 years; this was the tradition inherited by Irving (and continued by him from)
1878 to 1902. " (Byrne, p. 2.)

However, directly opposed to this tradition was Samuel Phelps who insisted upon simpler settings and better
texts in his productions at Sadler's Wells from 1844 to
1862. According to Miss Byrne, it was this philosophy
"from which the modern impulse derives," and it was
Phelps, more than anyone else before William Poel, who
did so much to restore a fuller Shakespearean text to the
stage. Taking his cue from Samuel Phelps, Frank R.
Benson, the director of the Shakespeare Memorial Theatre at Stratford during the last years of the century up
until the outbreak of World War I, used simplified though
realistically localizing sets. However, the chief criticism
of his settings was that they were not designed to permit
unbroken continuity of action. His real contribution to
the history of Shakespearean production appears to be the
creation and maintenance for a period of 30 years of a
Shakespearean repertory company which fostered the
love and knowledge of Shakespeare throughout England.

On the London stage Beerbohm Tree's production of
Julius Caesar in 1898 continued and enhanced the tradition
of opulant realism. Gordon Crosse in his Fifty Years of
Shakespearean Playgoing, published in 1940, recalls that,
seeing a Tree production, he once timed the intermissions
while the sets were being shifted and found that 45 minutes were lost. As an example of the treatment of the
texts, Tree omitted the whole of Act V, scene 2, of The
Winter's Tale. As a director I can sympathize with him,
for it is an almost entirely expositional scene of 188 lines
and, as such, is very difficult to stage. On the other
hand, it certainly seems necessary to the understanding

PRODUCING SHAKESPEARE

of the plot of the play and, moreover, provides opportunities for comedy which may emanate from Autolycus, the
Shepherd, and the Clown. The "ironic tone of The Times
review" of his production of Macbeth in 1911 gives us an
eloquent idea of Tree's distortions:

> Beauty is the thing this revival aims at, first
> and last. There is nothing ugly in the represen
> tation--not even the witches. . . . The sleep-
> walking scene was a scene of beauty. Flights
> of steps zig-zagged precipitously from the base
> to the very top of the scene. Evidently in an
> incident of sleep-walking it is appropriate that
> the sleep-walker should really have some walk
> ing to do. Lady Macbeth went slowly up and up,
> always beautifully. There was beauty again in
> the banqueting scene, barbaric beauty (including
> a fierce dance of retainers), and even the ghost
> of Banquo was a beautiful ghost. . . . Of course,
> we were never shaken with terror. Terror (on
> the stage) has had its day. (Byrne, p. 6.)

I might say parenthetically that though most present-day
producers of Macbeth seem to establish the proper mood
and atmosphere of the play they still insist on using
flights of steps which resemble those of either the Lincoln Memorial or the local court house. They, furthermore, seem to have little regard for the life and limbs
of the actors. On the opening night of the play a few summers or so ago at Stratford, Miss Diana Wynyard, playing Lady Macbeth, fell and injured herself because of the
maze of steps which formed the basis of the setting.

Nearly everything Beerbohm Tree stood for in Shakespearean production William Poel stood against. His
production of the First Quarto of Hamlet on an Elizabethan stage at St. George's Hall in 1881 was an eloquent rebellion against spectacle, realism in settings, and the
tampering with the texts. More important, it was a revealing demonstration that a play bore a vital relationship to the stage for which it was written. An article

appearing in the London Times Literary Supplement on
July 11, 1952, to commemorate his birth expresses Poel's
contribution to modern Shakespearean production.

> Like all true reformers, Poel went back to first
> principles. The integrity of the text, the conti-
> nuity of the action, the non-localized scene, the
> swift and musically inflected speech with the em-
> phasis on the key-word--these were the things he
> fought for. To playgoers accustomed to the real-
> istic splendours and slow pomp of Lyceum Shake-
> speare, and later the live rabbits and babbling
> brooks of Beerbohm Tree, Poel's gospel of poetic
> realism seemed an austere paradox. But there
> have been few important productions of Shake-
> speare during the past twenty-five years, at
> Stratford, the Old Vic or in the West End, which
> have not shown his influence.

> Poel's problem--the recreation of an Eliza-
> bethan performance within the limits imposed by
> the proscenium arch--was itself insoluble. . . .
> (However,) It has come increasingly to be seen
> that the shape of Shakespeare's theatre is as rel-
> evant to the presentation of his plays as the shape
> of the Attic theatre was relevant to the perform-
> ance of Greek tragedy. . . .

> The practice of his theory was often marred
> by eccentricity, and there was some justice in
> Archer's complaint that he was a "non-scenic
> Beerbohm Tree". He could be inconsistent with
> his own doctrine, ruthlessly cutting and trans-
> posing the texts which he held as sacrosanct. . . .
> But he performed the inestimable service of
> putting the Elizabethans back into their context,
> and of persuading us that they are all the more
> real for being allowed to speak for themselves.

Although Poel did not work in the professional theatre,

PRODUCING SHAKESPEARE

his theories were put into brilliant practice by Harley
Granville-Barker, whose production of The Winter's
Tale in 1912 was his first demonstration. Twelfth Night
and A Midsummer Night's Dream, as produced by him,
were memorable productions enlightened by the pioneer
work of Poel. Barker presented unabridged texts, speed-
ed up the tempo of performance, and insisted upon absolute fluidity of production. He also insisted upon ensem-
ble acting without "stars" and eliminated "conventional
cluttering" business. These were his main contributions
by way of practical, professional productions. However,
his lasting contribution to the director is, of course, his
most valuable Prefaces to Shakespeare.

To complete the narrative of the history of Shakespearean production in terms of important tendencies and
influences, it is necessary to mention the establishment
of the Old Vic in 1914, the work of the Birmingham Repertory Company under Sir Barry Jackson, and the Shakespeare Memorial Theatre under Bridges Adams. The
two latter theatres continued the practices of Granville-
Barker. Whereas the acting standard was higher at the
Old Vic, the use of scenery at Stratford was more imaginative. A definite landmark in production was Sir Barry
Jackson's modern-dress Hamlet, or "Hamlet in plus-
fours, " in 1925, antedating Orson Welles' production of
Julius Caesar by a number of years. When Sir Barry
Jackson presented this version in London at the Kings-
way Theatre, it was considered a "profoundly exciting"
experience for the average play-goer as well as the scholar and was unanimously praised by the best critics of the
day. Heretofore, to the conventional costuming of Hamlet had been added over the years an accumulation of conventional characterizations. Thus a change of dress
brought a fresh look to the play. Audiences and critics
seemed to be seeing and hearing the play for the first
time and were a little startled to find that it was a very
good play indeed. Even William Poel writing in the
Manchester Guardian seemed to feel that far from the
production's suffering from an absence of Elizabethan-
ism never had the "revenge motif been so well-handled

or made more explicit. " (Byrne, p. 12.) At least to the
mind of Muriel St. Clare Byrne Shakespeare in modern
dress is not (p. 13) " a mere stunt, an exercise in ingenuity" but a sincere attempt on the part of most producers
to find the "authentic Shakespeare. "

The advent of the modern-dress Hamlet, though apparently emphasizing a kind of physical production, actually
placed the emphasis on interpretation. It obviously had
"the drive and the sense of direction that only the producer's unifying concept can give. " (Byrne, p. 13.) Har-
court Williams' adherence to the Folio text at the Old Vic
from 1929 to 1933, his ignoring of all previous acting
versions with their cuts, scene divisions, and act divisions, his use of only one intermission, and his finding of
a ruling productional idea exemplified by his Jacobean
Midsummer Night's Dream and his Renaissance conception of Antony and Cleopatra, marked the pre-eminence
of the producer. By 1934 Harold Childe, the English
critic, lashing out at the producer, wrote: "At present
the age shows signs of wanting merely to find some way
of playing Shakespeare that has never been tried before
. . . and tricks are played with the construction and the
tone of the plays every whit as daring as those of Tate or
Cibber . . . The best possible base for all experiments
would be a strong and active tradition that Shakespeare,
as playwright, knew what he was about. " (Byrne, p. 15.)
He was writing for the most part in reaction to such highly stylized productions as Komisarjevsky's Macbeth and
The Merchant of Venice at Stratford in 1933. The obvious
change of period for some sophomoric reason like that of
desiring a shock effect on the audience--sheer sensation-
alism--certainly cannot be condoned. A change of period to create an extended chronological joke like the recent production of Love's Labour's Lost at the City Center should not escape censure. On the other hand, I saw
an entrancing production of the same play at Stratford in
1946 in the costumes and settings of Watteau which received unanimous approval by the critics because it
caught the pastoral quality of the play and at the same
time emphasized a gentle satirizing of the precious young

lords and ladies of that idyllic world. And I, for one, do not cavil at the recent productions of <u>Hamlet</u> at Stratford or the version presented by Maurice Evans which brought the costumes and locale of the play nearer to the present day. These productions, it seems to me, were not eccentric but gave "pictorial and emotional unity" (Byrne, p.16) to the play. They too placed the emphasis on interpretation and served to illuminate the texts for modern audiences.

In recent years the main trend of Shakespearean production has been characterized by a return to the full, uncut texts and an attempt to place them on a stage that bears a <u>resemblance</u> to the stage for which they were written. There has been a swing away from the purely theatrical to dramatic values. This means that modern producers are beginning to recognize the fact that the author knew his business. The concentration on matter rather than manner is the only way to synthesize drama with theatre.

Work done in England in the last 50 years or so has certainly influenced the theatre here. The visit of William Poel to Carnegie Tech, where he demonstrated his ideas on Elizabethan production, and the professional performances of Granville-Barker did much to clear away the cobwebs in the thinking in this country about producing Shakespeare. The ideas of Appia and Gordon Craig have affected the practice of designers like Norman Bel-Geddes, Robert Edmund Jones, Donald Oenslager, Lee Simonson, et al., and eliminated much of the superfluous detail of realism from Shakespearean production. However, beginning with Edwin Booth, our first really great Shakespearean actor and manager, Shakespearean production in America has been often spectacular and opulant. Booth in this country consciously or unconsciously was influenced by Henry Irving in England. He and other American producers naturally looked to Shakespeare's native England for guidance. Sothern and Marlowe continued the tradition. Jones' designs for <u>Hamlet</u>, <u>Richard III</u>, and <u>Macbeth</u> were among the first examples of imaginative conceptions of Shakespearean production. Since that time we have had other examples. However, alternating with this enlight-

McMULLAN

ened view, there has been an equal if not a greater number of elaborate, if not realistic, highly decorative productions. Twentieth-century Shakespearean productions on Broadway characteristically have been, in one way or another, designers' holidays. Fairly typical of what happens to Shakespeare when he is transported to the Broadway theatre is made clear by Brooks Atkinson's review ("Forest of Arden, " New York Times, February 19, 1950) of the Theatre Guild's production of As You Like It, of the not too dim past. He says:

> Most commercial Shakespearean productions are put on as if the producers were very much afraid that the audiences would not like Shakespeare. The plays and the actors are buried in scenery and pageantry. In the Katharine Cornell "Antony and Cleopatra" there was hardly room enough for an actor to cross the stage without barking his shins; and the same thing is true of "As you Like It," although Miss Hepburn's legs, as many transfixed students of art have pointed out, deserve every possible protection. Scene designers and costume designers take equal rank with actors in many commercial presentations of Shakespeare on Broadway.

Possessed of leaner pocketbooks and more adventuresome spirits than the Broadway angels, and wishing to learn from the past, the amateur university theatres have followed in the footsteps of William Poel and Granville-Barker. Here in the Department of Drama at Yale we have been influenced strongly by these two pioneers in our program of historical productions of Elizabethan drama. In 1938 we built an adaptation of an Elizabethan stage. Upon this stage we produced Marlowe's Edward the Second, Jonson's The Silent Woman, and Shakespeare's Richard III and Hamlet. It is about this production of Hamlet on this stage that I would like to speak, for it is the production of Shakespeare under these conditions which forms the basis of my ideas about the entire subject of producing Shakespeare. (Parts of the following discussion of the Yale <u>Hamlet</u> were published, with changes in wording, in <u>The Players Magazine</u>, April, 1942.)

As a director, I went back to first principles. I wanted to find out the advantages of the Elizabethan stage. At the outset, however, I decided that the production was not to be an attempt to represent an archeologically correct copy of an Elizabethan performance but rather that the production was to catch the spirit of an Elizabethan performance. Inasmuch as the set suggested only the characteristic form of the Elizabethan stage, the costumes were fundamentally Elizabethan in style and not exact in detail; the lighting was modified in the interest of the mood and variety desired from scene to scene. The directing and acting were, of course, dictated by the actor-audience relationship created by this particular stage; the action and business, while starting on the inner stage, were brought forward to the forestage as often as possible and the actors played out to the audience on important speeches, in the asides, and in the soliloquies. Movement and business were used only when essential and significant. Pictorial dramatizations were simple and slightly formal. A bench was placed on each side of the stage by court attendants before the performance began, and other properties were set and removed as needed. In general this approach served to establish the style of the production.

Though the chief characteristics of the Elizabethan stage are well known, it might be advisable at this point to describe its adaptation for the Yale University Theatre. The forestage was built to jut forward about 13 feet from the proscenium arch of our stage over 2 rows of orchestra seats and all the way across the auditorium, about 46 feet, to the side walls. One foot from the edge of our forestage was a door in each side wall of the theatre which permitted entrances onto the forestage. About 2 feet upstage from the proscenium arch was a door stage right and one stage left. The curtain for the inner stage was 17 1/2 feet from the edge of the forestage. The inner stage, with a door in either side wall and one in the back wall, was 6 feet deep and 13 feet wide. The balcony or upper stage was about 10 feet high, directly over the inner stage, and extended over the doors right and left which were 2 feet upstage from the proscenium arch.

One of the first problems facing the director using this stage was the determination of the playing areas for each scene.

At this point I want to digress a moment from a description of this production to discuss briefly certain theories that have been advanced regarding the director's use of the reconstruction or replica of the Elizabethan stage. These theories specifically concern staging in John Cranford Adams' Globe replica at Hofstra College. Writing in the March, 1953, issue of the Educational Theatre Journal (pp. 8-9), Bernard Beckerman, my friend and the director of plays at Hofstra, says:

> . . . what an Elizabethan stage--and particularly one of correct proportions--offers the director is an instrument whereby he can give the highly desirable continuity thematic significance as well as a dramatic form simple for the audience to follow. . . . Through the continuity it is necessary that the spectator understand the relation of one part to another, of one scene to the one before and the one after, as well as to the play as a whole. This the Globe stage is equipped to do by placing each scene in visual and dramatic relationship to every other in a pattern of movement which reflects the working out of the situation. . . . For example, the script of Twelfth Night embodies several plot lines which converge in a final, extended scene. . . .

> To reflect this pattern the director can place the romantic story on the platform . . . The earlier parts of the comic story are then played in the chamber. As the divergent strains

of the plot come together all the action is
brought to the platform. One of the results
is that clarity of plot is achieved. By associating each of the many characters with a
fixed locality an audience finds it easier to
identify each one until he or she becomes
more familiar. Another result is that the
pattern thus created holds the play together
as it flows from one area to another. Serving as a prologue, the first three scenes of
Twelfth Night illustrate how the continuity is
achieved on the Globe stage. Act I, Scene i
introduces a love-sick Orsino seated in . . .
the study. As he goes off to "beds of flowers,"
the curtain closes upon the study and Viola
enters from stage left accompanied by the
sea captain, learns she is in Illyria, and de-
parts stage right for Orsino's court. Over-
lapping her exit the upper curtain parts revealing Sir Toby and Maria . . . Here the
flow is continuous, one scene over-lapping
another, separating the strands of the story,
for when next we see Maria and Sir Toby they
will still be in the chamber.

While this is an interesting concept of staging, I must
take exception to it on the ground that it invalidates what
I consider to be the basic principle of the Elizabethan
stage, which is that it was constructed to create a poetic
theatre of the imagination and not a realistic theatre of
literal reproduction of actuality. It permitted not only
fluidity by elasticity. The insistence that "By associating
each of the many characters of a play with a fixed locality the audience finds it easier to identify each one" stems
from a concept which underlies the modern realistic theatre and denies the audience its use of the simplest and
easiest kind of imagination. Surely the identification of
characters in the plays of Shakespeare has little to do with
their association with particular physical aspects of the
Elizabethan stage. Surely they identify themselves by

their words, costumes, actions, and their relationships
to other characters in terms of their psychology and the
structure of the play. Does this mean that because the
audience has first seen Sir Andrew, Sir Toby, and Maria
in the upper stage or chamber they must be there when
they are next seen? I think, rather, that the audience
will believe who the characters say they are and where
they say they are by the persuasive force of their words
which, by their imagery, evoke personality and locality
more vividly and palpably than paint, plaster, and wood
or canvas.

Furthermore, literal localization and character association with it can be dramatically and theatrically suici-
dal. This was proved to me very forcibly when I saw a
production of Macbeth last spring on the Globe stage at
Hofstra. The Lady Macbeth sleep-walking scene was
played on the upper stage evidently because it connoted
her apartment. Even though it was technically well acted
and directed, the greater part of its effectiveness was
lost because of the height of the acting area and the physical distance between the actors and the audience. Surely the use of the forestage for the scene would have better
projected the nightmare aberrations of Lady Macbeth's
mind. The soliloquies of Macbeth, on the other hand,
which were played on the forestage, gained in clarity and
emotional impact by their sheer proximity to the audience.
In effect, audience identification and empathy with Macbeth were increased tremendously.

The noted American Shakespearean scholar who has
done so much work on the Elizabethan stage, George F.
Reynolds, writing in 1951 in Shakespeare Survey (pp. 98-9),
supports my view in his article "Was There a 'Tarras'
in Shakespeare's Globe?" He denies the absolute existence of this area by arguing against what he calls "the
underlying principle which causes Adams to look for a
tarras at all, and which motivates his entire book, "The
Globe Playhouse. It is, he says,

the idea that the more realistically and literally
every hint of stage directions and textual allu-

sions as to stage settings and equipment is carried out the better. Applying similar interpretations to the Elizabethans that one would to Ibsen or Pinero or any other realistic modern dramatist, Adams arrives at a detailed inventory of stage equipment and construction and tries for a naturalistic consistency easy for a modern reader to accept, but quite foreign not only to the Elizabethan stage but to that of the 18th century and the early 19th, as well . . . Not only does Adams's theory show a fundamental misunderstanding of Elizabethan stagecraft; it seems to indicate a misconception of dramatic illusion in general. This is a late date to have to insist that dramatic illusion has little to do with an illusion of reality . . .

Now, returning to our production of <u>Hamlet</u>, the text often indicated the stage areas to be used at a particular time. For example, it appeared obvious that the first scene should be played on the upper stage. Yet, Bernardo's and Francisco's opening lines suggested that, while Francisco was on the upper stage, Bernardo, for the sake of illusion, could not be there. Thus Bernardo was instructed to enter at the door down left on the forestage, see Francisco, challenge him, and then walk upstage and enter the up left door which led to the upper stage after the line, "'Tis now struck twelve"; and finish the line, "Get thee to bed, Francisco," as he arrived at the top of the balcony steps. After that Francisco went down the steps as he said, "Not a mouse stirring." Then Bernardo called down the speech, "If you do meet Horatio and Marcellus, the rivals of my watch," etc. By the time he had finished this speech, Horatio and Marcellus appeared on the forestage, entering from down right, Horatio going before Marcellus. They were therefore able to speak to Francisco and go up the steps to the balcony without a break in the dialogue. The scene continued in the middle section of the balcony until the appearance of the ghost in the stage right area of the balcony. The ghost reappeared in the stage left area and finally crossed in front of Horatio, Bernardo, and Marcellus on the central area and disappeared right. The scene ended with the exit of Horatio, Marcellus, and Bernardo.

The Council Chamber scene followed on the forestage. Laughing and chattering lords and ladies were "discovered," and Hamlet in his "inky cloak" was seated on a bench stage right. The King and Queen entered down right and ascended the throne placed in the inner stage before the beginning of the performance. At the exit of the court the inner stage curtains closed. Hamlet finished the scene on the forestage with his soliloquy and his subsequent promise to meet Horatio, Marcellus, and Bernardo at their watch that night.

After Hamlet's exit from the forestage the curtains of the inner stage were drawn once more to discover Ophelia and Laertes. They were joined by Polonius on the forestage where the scene continued until their exit from it.

When the lights dimmed on the forestage and came up on the balcony Hamlet and his friends were found there waiting for the ghost. The ghost appeared in the left area of the balcony and disappeared down the steps left with Hamlet in pursuit. The ghost was next seen in the inner stage as Hamlet entered onto the forestage from the door up left. When their scene ended with the closing of the inner stage curtains to blot out the ghost, Hamlet remained on the platform where he was ultimately joined by Marcellus and Horatio. After swearing silence to what they had seen, they went out down right.

Though the "parapet" scene began on the upper stage, it shifted to the platform and later to the inner stage. When the ghost left the upper stage he carried his locale with him: where the character says he is, or implies he is, there, in the minds of the audience, he is indeed. As the play progressed no "fixed locality" was reserved for particular characters. The characters moved with the ebb and flow of the structure of the play and found themselves wherever the tide of the dramatic imagination took them.

The play within the play scene demonstrates how the entire stage can be put to use. This scene, of course, presents a problem both in interpretation and in dramatization. As for interpretation in the present performance, it was decided that the dumb show should be eliminated because its presentation tended to lessen the suspense and created the debatable question of the King's reaction during its presentation. I reasoned that, although Dover Wilson's suggestions might be carried out, the dumb show would spring the trap too soon. For this reason it seemed better to go at once into the "play scene" and use it as a dramatic device to "catch the conscience of the King." With lords and ladies placed in the upper stage to watch the play, the problem was reduced to that of so strategically placing the King and Queen in one place and Hamlet in another that the audience could best direct its attention to them as the two main focal points and on the play within the play as the minor point of interest. Consequently it was decided to place the King and Queen up center in the inner stage on a raised throne, with Hamlet down right, and the play down left. The audience's attention could then go from one point to another with ease, with the King and Queen in the most prominent position.

Illusion of locale in terms of setting presented no obstacle to the six audiences which watched this production of Hamlet. Once the convention of the characters' indicating their whereabouts was boldly established at the beginning of the play, each locale was clearly defined. It proved that the more the spectator's imagination is encouraged to work, the more lively and active it becomes.

We may sum up the advantages in the use of the Elizabethan form of stage. It is quite plain that it allows a quick change of scene which gives the whole production fluidity. The over-all playing time for this production of the uncut Hamlet was 3 hours and 47 minutes, while that of the Margaret Webster-Maurice Evans production was closer to 5 hours, that of Benson in 1900 ran 4 1/2 hours, and that of the Old Vic 4 hours and 32 minutes. The time-consuming factor of most Shakespearean pro-

71

ductions is created by realistic sets which not only strongly localize the scenes but work against the cinematic,
structural blending of scene with scene. Shakespeare
used motion-picture technique in writing scenes in that
they do not build to climactic crescendos but dissolve
and fade into one another to create a cumulative effect.

For the poetically theatrical plays, operating on a
plane of heightened reality, Hamlet, Macbeth, Lear,
Othello, and Richard III particularly, I believe that a
kind of formal nonrealistic stage is necessary. (Some of
the comedies can be enhanced by a greater degree of pictorial detail.) Shakespeare must have realized the tem-
poral and auditory limitations of the theatre as an artistic form, and intended a simplicity and directness of ideas,
character, and action which could be grasped quickly and
directly.

Simplicity and directness of presentation are inevitably bound up with the problem of the aesthetic distance
between the audience and the play. Surely the open-air
innyard theatre of such a capacity to accommodate, according to De Witt, two to three thousand people, many
of whom were not seated, demanded the closest possible
proximity between the players and the audience if the audience were to hear and feel the emotional and intellectual impact of the play. The use of the forestage jutting
out into the audience permitted the actor to establish intimate contact. From my own experience with our Hamlet, I know that the soliloquies, delivered on the forestage, have never before or since so moved me. Identification and empathy with Hamlet were complete. Evidently this was Shakespeare's intention.

A great deal of modern scholarship has been devoted
to investigating Elizabethan stage conditions which, the
more we learn about them, tend the more to establish
principles which affect the dramatic intentions of the plays
and are instructive to the director. In the last year or
two, especially, there has been a flurry of excitement
over so-called discoveries. However, if I may be so bold,
I would urge a degree of caution in accepting every notion
proposed about the Elizabethan stage. A foot candle of

light may be focused on some heretofore darkened
area but the light is filtered foggily through speculation
rather than transmitted clearly through possible theatrical practice. For example, Mr. Leslie Hotson's ideas
about Shakespeare's stage being an "arena" stage or a
"theatre-in-the-round," as presented in the Sewanee Review, July, 1953, cause me, as a practical worker in the
theatre, to ask a few practical questions. As I understand him, he says that when the plays were presented at
court the stage was placed in the middle of the hall in order to permit Elizabeth to "see, hear, and be seen. " He
goes on to present records from the Office of Works which
indicate that they were responsible not only for construct-
ing a "broad stage in the middle of the Haull" but also
"making ready the Hall with degrees (tiers) with boards
on them. " This is certainly evidence that Shakespeare
was performed "in the round," but then Mr. Hotson dis-
cusses the question of settings and comes to the conclusion that "houses" or "mansions" were set before the play
began and were unchanged. Now, I know from practical
experience in working in the arena theatre, with an audience of nearly 400 sitting on tiers or bleachers on four
sides of the acting area, that practically no settings can
be used if all members of the audience are to see the performance. Certain units can be placed at one or more of
the four corners of the acting area where the actors or-
dinarily make their entrances, but they must be outside
the playing space. If any piece of scenery or furniture
or any architectural feature is used it must be low enough
to allow the audience sitting in the first rows all around
to see over it. If the houses or mansions Mr. Hotson
speaks of were small enough to permit the audience to
see the action on the stage they must have been so small
that in using them for entrances or exits the actors must
have had to crawl through them--unless they were mid-
gets, and I don't recall that Burbage, Kemp, and the
other actors of Shakespeare's company were. On the other
hand, perhaps his assumption is correct that the stage
was placed in the middle of the hall in order to allow
Elizabeth to "see, hear, and be seen. " If so, I would

say that a large number of her court could not. Perhaps
that did not matter. I suspect it didn't.

Certainly scholars who have attempted to find out the
physical conditions of the stage for which Shakespeare
wrote have contributed enormously to our understanding
of the plays. Every playwright in the history of the theatre has written for the stage and conventions of the time.
The recent movement back to the Elizabethan stage must
be greeted with loud bravos. An understanding of how the
stage was used is necessary to the producer if he is to
project the dramatic and poetic qualities of Shakespeare's
plays. We shall forever be beholden to Granville-Barker
for helping us to a better understanding because he has
brought us the knowledge of the scholar and the practical
producer who worked in terms of the stage for which
Shakespeare wrote. However, it must be emphasized
that he himself did not, for the most part, produce Shakespeare on a replica Shakespearean stage. Instead he used
a formal, pictorial stage which utilized the _form_ of the
Shakespearean stage. The form of this stage, in my opinion, is more important to the modern producer than a
replica of the stage.

The Elizabethan stage actually has some disadvan-
tages. Sightline limitations and the lack of levels, except
that created by the balcony, are hindrances to visual
dramatization. I have found that the inner stage, because
of its distance from the audience and poor sightlines for
those seated at the extreme right and left of the house,
can be used merely to start a scene, with the actors playing within a small triangle of space, and then the actors
have to be brought forward to the forestage. The inner
stage can be used, as Miss Margaret Webster points out
in her _Shakespeare Without Tears_, (New York, McGraw-
Hill, 1942, p. 55) only as a "jumping-off place for a scene
in which standing furniture or props had to be 'discovered',
and that the main action must have been brought forward
as soon as possible to the main stage itself." The use of
levels in our modern scheme of "space staging" gives the
director many opportunities for variety of movement and
pictorial effect denied by the Elizabethan stage. The

PRODUCING SHAKESPEARE

upper stage, because of its height and its distance from
the audience, presents sightline problems and is a poor
area for scenes demanding intimate audience contact. The
absence of a front curtain forces the producer to have
actors "Take up the bodies" while others march off. As
Miss Webster says, "There is no sense in pretending that
this is not, flatly, an ineffective and clumsy necessity with
which Shakespeare did the best he could."

Brooks Atkinson, writing in the New York Times,
August 23, 1953, described his reactions to the stage
used at Antioch College for its Shakespearean festival.
He starts out by saying:

> There is one thing this summer in America
> has proved: To see Shakespeare plain you have
> to see him on a platform stage. . . . For it is
> time we pulled loose completely from the gran-
> diose pretensions of the 19th century style of
> Shakespearian producing. It is time we came
> face to face with the plays.

> One reason for the general success of the
> Antioch Area Theatre Festival has been the
> platform stage . . . Here the plays move fast
> and the actors do not fritter away energy in
> externals of showmanship.

> Whatever the Globe stage was like in de-
> tail, it brought the plays and the audience to-
> gether in a compact unity . . .

Then he goes on to criticize the Antioch stage because it
is so huge and rambling, and defeats the purpose of
bringing the audience close to the play.

His summarizing paragraph is most important to us
because in it he says: "It is the essence of Shakespeare
that today fascinates audiences who for the first time
are getting . . . into the heart of the dramas. At present the essence is somewhat diffused at Antioch on a
stage that is too general in design. There must be some

way of retaining the freedom of a platform stage without
losing intimacy of performance. "

This last sentence gets at the truth of the matter, I
think. The point is that the essence of Shakespeare can
best be projected by "retaining the freedom of a platform
stage without losing intimacy of performance. "

The modern theatre is perfectly well able to create
the physical conditions of production which will gain the
simplicity of background, freedom, speed, continuity,
and proximity of the Elizabethan stage. It may mean
breaking through the proscenium arch and eradicating
the picture frame to make closer contact with the audience. It means less use of scenery as such and more use
of lighting which can, by suggestion and poetic means,
establish the illusion of locale and the emotional climate
of Shakespeare's plays. A reversion to the primitive
stage of Shakespeare is not necessary. This, in my opinion, would be a myopic view of the value of historical
scholarship. It surely does not urge literal duplication
of the original conditions under which the plays were produced.

Shakespeare's plays can be performed on a reconstructed Elizabethan stage, but the reaction of the audience can be only that of the 20th century. All efforts to
transplant an audience to the days of Elizabeth and
James I will color very little the emotional and mental
attitudes of today. Even antiquarian inspired attempts
to dress up members of the audience and put some of
them on the stage cannot create much more than the atmosphere of a masquerade ball. The trouble is, of
course, that there aren't enough costumes to dress the
entire audience and those on stage in costume simply remove themselves farther from the rest and become actors. Those in mufti can see the whole production only
objectively and become further removed aesthetically
from the play. Such efforts at archeological productions
of Shakespeare call attention to themselves and defeat
their purposes. Rather than influencing the audiences'
imagination they become distracting. Belasco's attempts
to establish an oriental atmosphere for an oriental play

by burning incense perhaps helped the mood of the actors but succeeded only in setting off fits of coughing among the audience. The frying of bacon and the boiling of coffee in his Child's restaurant transplanted onto the stage merely made the audience hungry. The sight of blood dripping from the meat of the butcher's shop on the stage of André Antoine's Théâtre Libre merely made the ladies faint and the men seek the nearest exit. The theatre is a place of the imagination and not actuality. Historical knowledge of the actual conditions of Shakespearean production must be <u>distilled</u> to find the essence of Shakespeare. His true substance or the "inward nature underlying its manifestations" must be conveyed to modern audiences in terms of the present.

This can be achieved only by the continued collaboration of scholarship and the theatre. The lion and the lamb --and here we don't have to make the delicate distinction as to who is what--must lie down together to share knowledge and experience to make William Shakespeare "of an age and for all time. "

Arleigh D. Richardson, III

THE EARLY HISTORICAL PLAYS

"There is a history in
all men's lives. "

--2 <u>Henry IV</u> (3.1.80)

February 24, 1954

Shakespeare's early histories are, in some ways, the most controversial works of the entire Shakespeare canon. In fact, so controversial are they that they have suffered the usual fate of children whose origins are questioned. Groups of scholars on the one hand have pushed them forward as the legitimate offspring of Shakespeare's genius, while others have averted their faces in embarrassment, stoutly denying the possibility that the bard could ever have strayed so far from the path of virtue as to beget such monsters. The doubt thus cast upon their origin has caused these plays to be unduly neglected for the most part in recent years, both by the general reader and by the theater. Such neglect, I feel, is unfortunate.

I should like to consider with you today some of the vexing questions which surround the early plays, particularly those of the <u>Henry VI</u> trilogy. I should like to discuss their background, the circumstances of their origin, and their significance, suggesting to you why I feel that although undeniably weaker than many of their brethren, they deserve, nonetheless, our respectful attention.

First of all, let us review some of the facts which Mr. Harding pointed out in his lecture of this series. It has long been a commonplace that Londoners in the last decades of the 16th century were great theater goers. It is perfectly true, of course, that the theater flourished magnificently during that period. But the careful estimates of Professor Alfred Harbage are interesting indeed. After a thorough study of such contemporary records as Henslowe's <u>Diary</u>, he makes the

conservative estimate that in 1595 about 2,500 people a
day, or 15,000 a week, on an average, were attending
the theater in London. Estimating the population of London at the time is a difficult matter; but again after careful study of the extant records, Professor Harbage suggests that 13% of the population, or two persons in fifteen
went to the theater each week. Not a very large proportion, when one recalls that bear-baiting, cock-fighting
and an occasional execution were about the only other
forms of organized entertainment.

Furthermore, although it would be foolish to insist
that it was the exact same 13% of the population which
went every week, nevertheless, the indications are that
probably about two-thirds of the London people never attended the theater at all. The fact that audiences nearly
doubled in size on the day of the opening of a new play
certainly argues a group of habitual playgoers. Obviously, the best reason for selecting a new play to see is that
the spectator has seen all the old ones.

Perhaps it is not entirely relevant, but it is certainly the stuff of dreams to think that London workmen and
their women, who made up the bulk of the audience, paid,
as a middle price, the equivalent of roughly seventy-five
cents to see a first performance of <u>Macbeth</u>, or to see
Will Shakespeare himself play as one of the leads in Jonson's <u>Everyman in his Humour</u>.

Now think, for a moment, of the way in which plays
ran. Henslowe's accounts for the running of his theater,
The Rose, show that an average run consisted of about
twelve performances spaced a week or so apart, usually with the first six showing higher than average receipts, and the second six lower; again the impression
conveyed being of a quickly exhausted clientele. Sometimes it required only a second or third performance
to send receipts below average, in which case, the
company withdrew its "turkey". On the other hand, the
repeated performances of old favourites like <u>Faustus</u>
testify to the willingness of playgoers to see some plays
more than once.

82

THE EARLY HISTORICAL PLAYS

Henslowe's theater was a large one, and a different play had to be supplied every afternoon. If the play was successful, it might be repeated later in the week, but a run of 22 performances for even the most successful play was uncommon. In general, there was a steady stream of new scripts, and Henslowe counted on novelty and a rapid turn-over to keep his theater filled with paying customers. Other owners must certainly have done the same. So numerous were the plays that Sir Philip Sidney felt compelled to devote a very long passage to the stage in his <u>Defense of Poesie</u> in 1580. He concludes his criticism with the statement:

> But I have lavished out too many words on this play matter. I do it, because as they are excelling parts of poesy, so is there none so much used in England ... Other sorts of poetry almost have we none, but that lyrical kind of songs and sonnets.

(And one might add, thank God too for those songs and sonnets).

We can easily see, then, that while the theater did of a certainty flourish in 16th century London, it depended on a relatively small part of the population for its support, and that these supporters created a constant demand for new plays. Such a demand, indicated by the receipts for opening performances, was obviously passed on from managers like Henslowe, with a good eye for business, to the playwrights who wrote for them.

Now these playwrights were abundantly prolific. Shakespeare's average output of better than one play a year was comparatively low. During the four years when he worked for Henslowe, Thomas Dekker turned out nearly a script a month, and Michael Drayton produced seventeen in a single year. And yet the tremendous demand for scripts was still hard for them to meet. The managers wheedled, threatened, and paid in advance to get plays. Henslowe was constantly making advance payments. Ben Jonson, for example, received

from him four pounds in 1597, probably an advance on
Everyman in his Humour. Nor were the playwrights always scrupulously honest by our present day standards.
Robert Greene sold the same play to two companies, and
it is a matter of record that managers hired writers to
refurbish old plays, the reason obviously being that for
less money than it had to pay for a completely new play,
a company could have an old one, already in its possession, modernised, and could then advertise it as new.
When William Cartwright, the actor, brought before the
Master of the Revels an old play which was to be produced at The Fortune, he asked for authorization to add
scenes for the express purpose, as Sir Henry Herbert
noted in his account book, "to give it out for a new one",
a reason which seemed natural to the Master of the Revels, for he gave the permission. And D. Lupton was
somewhat, shall we say, more blunt when he wrote in
his London and the Countrey Carbonadoed and Quarter-
ed:

> The players are as crafty with an old
> play, as bauds with old faces, the one puts
> on a new fresh colour, the other a new face
> and name.

There is a somewhat analogous situation in our own
entertainment world. Ruth McKenny published a book in
1939 entitled My Sister Eileen. For fifteen years it has
been running more or less continuously as a Broadway
play, a vastly successful movie, a radio and then a television series, and finally, of course, as the musical
comedy Wonderful Town, for which I defy anyone here
to get seats at the present moment.

If my account of the popularity of the theater, the
demand for new plays, and the practice of rewriting old
ones in 16th century London seems obvious to you, I do
not apologise. For it is just that quality of obviousness
which I want to emphasize. The whole matter seems so
obviously natural that one can only wonder at the elaborate attempts of some scholars during the last twenty

odd years to blind themselves to it, to seize Boreas by the dewlaps and wander down labyrinthine paths to other more complicated accounts of the way in which things happened. It seems curious indeed that people should be so exceedingly anxious to deny that Shakespeare could have begun his writing career by rewriting old plays, especially when one of the best known facts about Shakespeare's method (mentioned in every Freshman paper on Shakespeare) is that he never really originated a main plot, but merely rewrote, giving his golden touch to what was often pedestrian stuff.

As both Mr. Harding and Mr. Kokeritz pointed out, Shakespeare was a man, a human being with human emotions, desires and aspirations. He worked for his living, and being successful, he was able to achieve certain of his ambitions--returning to buy the largest house in Stratford, for example. He would not have been a financial success had he not written to please his audience, and his early experience at doing so was almost certainly by revising old plays. His company must have thought itself fortunate indeed--not of course at having in its midst one of the most inspired writers of the ages, but at having a Johannes fac totum, a Jack-of-all-trades, as Robert Greene scornfully termed him; an actor who could get top billing and who, as a member of the company, would polish up its old plays or plays already published, thereby obviating in many cases at least, the necessity to hire some hack like Greene to do the job.

What then, were the plays being produced to meet the great demand? We all know that there were many and diverse dramatic forms. There is evidence that some of the old moralities and interludes were still being performed in parts of England at the same time that the great romantic comedies, the tragedies, the Roman plays, and the histories, which we term Elizabethan were being presented. But by far the most popular on the London stage in its day was the history play, and by that term I include all those plays which drew their chief subject matter from the historical lore of the national chronicles. Between 1562 and the closing of the theaters in 1642 there is record of more than 150 plays dealing with subjects drawn from the history of England and from what went for such at that time. This number strongly suggests that around 25% of the plays written were histories.

One of these history plays was published as an anonymous quarto in 1594, entitled:

> The First Part of the Contention betwixt
> the Two Famous Houses of Yorke and Lancaster, With the Death of the Good Duke Humphrey; and the Banishment and Death of the Duke of Suffolke. And the Tragicall End of the Proud Cardinall of Winchester, With the Notable Rebellion of Jack Cade: And the Duke of Yorke's First Claime Unto the Crowne.

Aside from giving this rather ample title, the title page is sadly uncommunicative. It only tells us further that the play was printed in London by Thomas Creed for Thomas Millington, to be sold at his shop under Saint Peter's in Cornwall--no author, and no indication as to what company had owned it. In 1595, however, the same man, Thomas Millington, brought out another play entitled The True Tragedy of Richard Duke of Yorke. This quarto's title page discloses the fact that the play was "sundrie times acted by the Right Honourable the Earle of Pembrooke his servants". Now The True Tragedy is definitely a continuation of The Contention chronologically. The very title, The First Part of The Contention, implies a second part. Stylistically, the two have a great deal in common. And furthermore, another quarto, published in 1619, called The Whole Contention contains both plays and refers to them as two parts of the same play. It therefore seems perfectly reasonable to assume that The Contention as well as the True Tragedy belonged to the company known as The Earl of Pembroke's servants, a company which was forced into the provinces by the plague, and returned to London in dire financial straits in 1594, probably the reason for their selling scripts to the publishers.

THE EARLY HISTORICAL PLAYS

The late Professor Feuillerat has demonstrated how the mixture of styles in <u>The Contention</u> brands it as a play already revised once, probably having its real origin in the early 1580's. It is my belief that probably Robert Greene produced <u>The Contention</u> by refurbishing the older play. And the indications are that it was being played in London in 1591 or 1592.

In 1623, when Heminge and Condell, two of Shakespeare's fellow actors, brought out the First Folio containing all of Shakespeare's plays which they could assemble, it included the three parts of <u>Henry VI</u>. Parts two and three contain many close similarities to <u>The Contention</u> and <u>The True Tragedy</u> respectively. Their general structure and the ordering of events are closely alike, and in many cases the later plays contain whole passages which are identical with passages in the earlier two. The relationship between the two later plays, claimed for Shakespeare by men of his own company whose word there is no reason to doubt, and the earlier two versions has been the subject of dispute ever since the 18th century.

The theory which has been in vogue from some twenty years ago until almost the present is that of the memorial reconstructionists, who have maintained that <u>The Contention</u> and <u>The True Tragedy</u> represent pirated versions of Shakespeare's plays, the accurate versions of which appear in the Folio. By elaborate argument they have endeavoured to show that the two earlier versions are shorter and contain many differences in text because they were reconstructed for the printer by pirates who simply could not remember all the lines from a theater performance, and who had, therefore, at times to omit sections and to invent words, phrases, and lines to eke out their faulty memories.

The facts that booksellers and printers were not above pirating plays and that there were no copyright laws in Shakespeare's day, have stood the memorial reconstructionists in good stead.

Professor Prouty first, however, and I subsequently have carefully compared <u>The Contention</u> and <u>Henry VI</u>

Part II from nearly every possible point of view. The evidence that The Contention is not a pirated version of
Shakespeare's play is overwhelming. There is not time
now to go into many intricate details, nor do I wish to
bore you, but let me just cite one example. Certain
passages in Shakespeare's version can be shown to have
come from the second edition of Holinshed's chronicle
and from nowhere else. The chief sources of The Contention are the earlier chronicles of Grafton and Hall.
In The Contention there is not a single incident which
needs must come from Holinshed. Grafton, Hall and a
few identifiable miscellaneous sources for isolated inci-
dents are the reference works of the men who wrote and
rewrote The Contention. Holinshed was apparently not
used. It would be a curious argument indeed to have to
maintain that a pirate consistently omitted in his reconstruction each and every passage based on Holinshed.
Is it not much more sensible to conclude that the folio
version is a third version of the old play, a version done
by a writer who made use of Holinshed for certain epi-
sodes which he added? And since the folio editors attrib-
ute Henry VI Part II to Shakespeare, and Shakespeare
relied constantly on Holinshed for his historical material,
it seems a perfectly natural and sound conclusion that
Shakespeare took over an old play, The Contention, already revised once, and made of it his own version, now
known to us as Henry VI Part II.

Thus far I have dwelt mostly on the second part of
the trilogy. Detailed studies by Professor Feuillerat and
Alvin Kernan, a graduate student in our department, tend
to show that exactly the same relationship exists between
The True Tragedy and Henry VI Part III. Since Part I
exists only in the folio version, there is nothing with
which to compare it, and current theory, pretty well sub-
stantiated, has it that Shakespeare did Part I at a somewhat later date to capitalize on the popularity of the other
two. It is not necessary to the general unity of the trilogy, and indeed it fails to dovetail into the structure in
anything like the way the other two fit together.

For one thing, its setting is mostly France, while

the locale of Parts II and III is entirely England, with
only one scene across the channel. Part I contains details which are inconsistent with Parts II and III, and
which an author writing II and III after Part I could be
expected to have taken into account. For example, in
part I Henry is represented as old enough to be crowned
soon after his father's death, and to fall in love at the
end of the play. In Parts II and III mention is made
three times of the fact that he was only nine months old
at the time of his accession. Furthermore, Humphrey,
Duke of Gloucester, is a proud, quarrelling, stubborn
noble in Part I, while in Part II he is the good old man
who tries in vain to help Henry be a good King. It is also
strange that Talbot, the patriotic hero of Part I, and the
character who by contemporary accounts had a great
deal to do with the popularity of that play, is never once
mentioned in the other two parts.

All these details and others besides would seem to
indicate that Part I was a separate play, revised by
Shakespeare some time after he had done the other two,
and while I do not wish to do it an injustice, I feel that it
actually does little more for the trilogy than function as
a sort of preface. Dover Wilson believes that it depended for its popularity not only on its connection with Parts
II and III, but also on Essex's ill-fated expedition to
France and his siege of Rouen, to which there are many
parallels in the play. The whole question of its origin
and its relationship to the rest of the trilogy needs further study. Because of these unresolved questions and
because of its relative unimportance to the trilogy as a
whole, I ask your indulgence if I concentrate my re-
marks primarily on Parts II and III.

Such then is the background of the plays as far as
Shakespeare is concerned. They seem quite definitely
to represent the early efforts of Shakespeare, the novice, rewriting older plays for his company before he
branched out on his own. This was Malone's theory
some 164 years ago, but in the intervening years it had
become "sicklied o'er with the pale case of thought"
about pirates and memorial reconstruction.

RICHARDSON

If, as I maintain, the early histories are the works of the novice Shakespeare, what then is the tradition within which he first tried his hand at dramatic work? I have already pointed out the popularity on the London stage of works dealing with English history. Various studies by Tillyard, Dover Wilson, Una Ellis-Fermor, and others in recent years have been devoted to the history play tradition. As a result of their work, it is certainly no longer satisfactory in the least just to say that the chronicle plays of Shakespeare's time simply presented to the audience a slice of history with its opportunity for a brave show of rich costumes, noble personages, far off things, and battles long ago. Of course, the plays do that most successfully, but such splendid effects were, in a sense at least, the sugar coating of the pill, for history in the Tudor period, as indeed at other times, was meant to teach important lessons.

Not long after the conclusion of the long and bitter civil broils known as the Wars of the Roses, when Henry VII ascended the throne on somewhat shaky pretences, he was fortunate enough to find visiting his realm a gifted Italian, Polydore Vergil. The shrewd Henry, realizing the value of propaganda, commissioned Vergil to write a chronicle of the recent wars, the chief point of which of course, would be the glorification of the new monarch who, as the scion of both rival houses, Lancaster and York, was obviously destined by the working out of Fate, or Almighty God, to achieve the longed-for peace.

Vergil, obeying the wishes of his royal patron, became the ultimate source of the later chronicles which took up his thesis and embroidered upon it. For history, like all literature, according to Renaissance theory, must teach. And so Hall, in particular, designed a monumental work on a plan as classical in its balance as any 18th century masterpiece, depicting the process of fate, the turning of the wheel of fortune, in the greatest affairs of state and statesmen. He called his work, The Union of the Noble and Illustre Families of Lancaster & York. This particular chronicle was respon-

sible even more than the others for the propagation of
what has been called the Tudor Myth, that is, the historical "proof" that the civil wars were a kind of expiation for the sins of past rulers, an expiation, which having run its course, would lead to the restoration of
peace and stability and the founding of a new royal line
under Henry VII.

Another tradition lies behind the history plays too--
that of the morality plays. A. P. Rossiter has pointed
out in his edition of Thomas of Woodstock, an anonymous
play closely related to The Contention, that the inherent
medievalism of the Tudor mind kept the Morality pattern
alive and formative beneath all the Renaissance trap-
pings of story, phrase and character. It was perfectly
natural that on the stage didacticism should follow patterns evolving in the line of descent from the Moralities,
through the Interludes. The fact of the matter is that
most of the histories, and especially Shakespeare's development of the type, have drawn upon the didactic tradition of the Moralities, combining with it the moral
contained in the Tudor myth presented by the chroni-
clers. So one finds in the Henry VI plays not only the
beginning of the Lancaster-York factional broils, but a
clearly marked distinction between the good characters
such as Humphrey of Gloucester, representing old and
established values, and the bad characters, like the am-
bitious and proud York.

Other forms of literature enter the picture as well.
Lily B. Campbell has made it quite clear that A Mirror
for Magistrates, published in many editions from 1559 -
1610, played a very influential part in the literary world,
providing material for countless plays, including the
ones with which we are concerned today. A Mirror, as
its title implies, was unabashedly didactic, endeavour-
ing to show men in lofty places how their greatness of
position is utterly dependent upon the working of fate,
and how often great men and women have gone from
high to low as a result of some moral flaw in their conduct. A Mirror, as well as the chronicles, provided
historical source material, already moralized, so to

speak, for countless historical plays. At least 25 of its sections dramatize characters conspicuous in Shakespeare's plays, not to mention those of other histories.

As Renaissance man became more secularized, and as his curiosity began to range, speculation soon turned from abstract problems of morality and religion to more concrete problems including that of government. A Mirror is not only important as a source of much material used by the playwrights. It is even more important as a sign of the times. Its popularity indicates to us better than anything else the significance of the problem of morality in government which occupied much of Tudor thought, and which appears very specifically not only in The Contention, but also in the whole of Shakespeare's trilogy and his other history plays as well. In fact, once we set foot along this path of preoccupation with the problem of morality in high places and the duties and responsibilities of rulers, we are off on the highroad leading to the great tragedies which came much later in Shakespeare's career. There is a definite evolution from the studies of kingship in the history plays where the focus is chiefly on the office itself to the study of human reactions and flaws in the kings and rulers of the later tragedies, Macbeth, Lear, Othello, Antony and Cleopatra, and, of course, Hamlet.

Consider for a moment the other early plays. Love's Labour's Lost with its great artificiality of language is direct imitation of John Lyly. The Comedy of Errors is Shakespeare's version of Plautine comedy. Two Gentlemen of Verona is partly from Montemayor's Diana and is in the very common Renaissance tradition of the friendship theme. Titus Andronicus is clear and obvious Senecan imitation. It is only in the early histories that we find the beginnings of a preoccupation with morality and human character in high places which leads to such questions as that concerning the actions of Brutus, the honorable man, in Julius Caesar.

If it was revision which started Shakespeare on this path, then I ask again, do we need to feel ashamed for him?

THE EARLY HISTORICAL PLAYS

<u>Henry VI</u> Parts II and III have seemed to some
people a mere jumble of events taken from the chronicles and paraded on the stage. Actually to the Elizabethan, and to us if we look with unbiased eyes, the
main theme is quite apparent. For as the title tells us,
the two plays deal mainly with the reign of the good
man and bad king, Henry VI, whose weakness as a ruler
makes him a fit object for didacticism in the best <u>Mirror
for Magistrates</u> vein. In a like manner, one sees the
wheel of fortune--that favourite symbol, working in the
affairs of every major figure of both plays. In <u>Henry VI</u>
Part II, Humphrey, Duke of Gloucester, Eleanor his
Duchess, Suffolk, Cardinal Beaufort and Somerset are
all at the top of the wheel as the play opens, and all are
cast down before it ends. In <u>Henry VI</u> Part III, York,
Henry, Queen Margaret and Warwick are all cast down.
To be sure, the wheel turns faster for some than for
others, but one is never allowed to lose the sense of its
inexorable turning.

One does not have to look far for the unifying thread
in these last two plays of the trilogy. It is, of course,
the King himself, and the great question central to the
trilogy is what can be done with an unsuccessful ruler.
I was about to say a bad ruler, but one of Henry's chief
characteristics is his goodness. Even Warwick, Henry's
enemy at the time, speaks of him as "famed for mild-
ness, peace and prayer". Throughout the two plays he
is the embodiment of Christian virtue, but that does not
make him a good King. In that position his very virtues
turn to faults. He is blinded to treachery and evil in
others, and as a result he becomes a pawn in the political game played by his Queen, Richard of York, and the
two factions led by the red rose and the white. Continually ruled by those around him, he makes disgraceful
terms for the possession of his wife when he gives away
most of the France so gloriously won by his father. He
is popular with no one. His common subjects are all
too ready to rise against him in a Cade rebellion, or to
take the Yorkist side when the future for the Lancasters
looks black, yet he genuinely feels great sorrow for

93

their plight. Witness the battle of Towton scene where, while he is wishing he were a country swain, having been chided from the battle by the Amazonian Margaret, he witnesses the symbolical scene in which a father discovers he has killed his own son, and a son discovers that he has killed his own father. Henry says:

> O piteous spectacle! O bloody times!
> Whiles lions war and battle for their dens,
> Poor harmless lambs abide their enmity.
> Weep, wretched man, I'll aid thee tear
>   for tear;
> And let our hearts and eyes, like civil
>   war,
> Be blind with tears, and break o'ercharged
>   with grief.
>   .   .   .
>
> Was ever king so grieved for subject's woe?
> Much is your sorrow; mine ten times so much.
> Sad hearted men, much overgone with care,
> Here sits a king more woeful than you are.

And from the time that Henry lets Gloucester fall into the hands of his enemies, he is surrounded by almost no prominent character who is not driven by ambition. Eleanor of Gloucester, Richard of York, Queen Margaret, Jack Cade, Somerset, Suffolk, Beaufort, York's sons, Edward, George and Richard, and Warwick; every one of them is spurred on to dire actions by sheer ambition. Against this setting, Henry seems a saint indeed, but a saint is not a good king. As if this point needs to be driven home again and again in the plays, Henry is shown doing things which would make it doubly clear to his audience. He sits idly by while good old Gloucester is ruined by his enemies. He gives away France, as I have already mentioned; he signs away his own son's right to the throne; he finally makes Warwick and Clarence Lords Protector of the realm, resigning the rule himself, and to make matters worse

he turns over the government to Warwick who has been
one of his most bitter enemies. Henry's flaws as a ruler are obvious indeed.

Why then must those who oppose him and try to pull
him off the throne be portrayed as villains? It would
seem that in the case of so ruinous a rule, they might be
justified in replacing Henry, whose claim is rather ques-
tionable anyhow, with a man who might do a much better
job, and bring order out of chaos. But there's the rub.
Many of you will remember that Mr. Harding spoke of
the Elizabethans' dislike of social change. And an
anointed monarch, though his claim be clouded, is the
great symbol not only of authority, but of universal order, and no matter how badly he may perform his duties,
it is a hazardous thing to even contemplate his removal.
Chaos may come again. The question of what is right
and proper in a case like Henry's becomes then a sore
one, one with which the Elizabethan mind was greatly
preoccupied.

A whole series of history plays of roughly the same
date as the trilogy testifies to the fact that the playwrights
were concerned with the idea, and if they were, it is
surely logical to suppose that their audiences were as
well. Marlowe's Edward II, the anonymous Thomas of
Woodstock, the Henry VI trilogy, Richard III and
Richard II, not to mention The Contention and the True
Tragedy were, despite controversy about dates, all
written within the same decade, and they are all very
closely related in their concentration on the theme of
authority, in their study of kings unsuited in one way or
another to rule. Each one of these is what A. P. Rossiter
calls a moral history, one which has allegorized the
events found in the chronicles even beyond their state
in the source material, juggling the historical details
which they treat in such a way as to bring out some particular point.

One important question remains for us to consider
here. Do these plays have any relevance today? Can
they be anything more to us than interesting literary
fossils?

RICHARDSON

Perhaps one clue to the answer lies in the fact that recent productions of the early histories have been eminently successful. The Birmingham Repertory Theatre produced <u>Henry VI Part II</u> on April 3, 1951, and <u>Henry VI Part III</u> on April 1, 1952. The same group took the latter to the Old Vic in July 1952, and performed the entire trilogy as part of the Coronation festivities last summer in London. Sir Barry Jackson of the Birmingham theatre, had this to say about the plays:

> The dissection of the text and the implica-
> tion that it is not entirely Shakespeare's I must
> leave to the scholars in their cloistered nooks,
> but what is as clear as daylight from the prac-
> tical view of stage production is that the author
> was a dramatist of the first rank, though per-
> haps immature. If the author was not Shake-
> speare, I can only regret that the writer in
> question did not give us more examples of his
> genius. In short, <u>Henry VI</u> is eminently actable.

In speaking of the scene I have already mentioned, in which the King witnesses the father who has killed his son and the son who has killed his father, Sir Barry has this to say:

> Though we know that family cleavages of
> such a tragic nature occurred in Germany dur-
> ing our own lifetime and that the parricides
> were not even accidental, Shakespeare's direc-
> tions, when read, easily raise a smile. Rather
> than run the risk of a laugh in the audience, we
> discussed omitting the incident altogether. The
> poet's infallible intuition, however, proved right.
> The scene was retained but treated as a static
> tableau: it shone out away and above the violent
> episodes with which it is surrounded and threw
> more light on the horror of civil war than all
> the scenes of wasteful bloodshed. The still fig-
> ures of the father and son speaking quietly and

    unemotionally, as though voicing the thoughts
    that strike the saintly, sad King's conscience,
    presented a moment of calm and terrible re-
    flection.

Certainly the company did well to retain that scene, for
it symbolizes the central theme of the trilogy.
    Here, then, is evidence not only that the plays are
actable, but that a modern audience, somewhat to the
producer's surprise, gathers at least something of the
central meaning of the work, just as the Elizabethan
audience must have done.
    In New York last Fall the New York City Center pre-
sented a revival of Richard III directed by Margaret
Webster, with Jose Ferrer in the title role. That Miss
Webster saw in it something more than just a bit of
dramatized ancient history was made clear when at one
point a swastika was projected upon the walls of the
Tower of London--in my humble opinion a gratuitous bit
of commentary, but nonetheless indicative.
    One might also mention, at least, the revival of
Maurice Evans' production of Richard II on television
last month, a revival which that commercially minded
medium would never have considered, had it not thought
of the play as timely.
    It seems to me that upon consideration, our answer
as to the relevance of the early histories today must be
in the affirmative. One hesitates to say that history re-
peats itself, but there were many aspects of the Elizabethan world which made it similar to our own. The
background against which we live out our lives is just
as chaotic as the Elizabethans'. Their fear lest the
bloody days of the Wars of the Roses return was probably no less strong than the atmosphere of terror which
prompts men to hysterical behavior today.
    And surely no one will deny that the two ages are
closely akin in their serious questioning of authority, its
rights and responsibilities. Substitute for the term king
any word you choose--President, Dictator, Premier,
Chairman. Strip these plays for the moment of their

quaintness, of their pageantry, and you will find underneath questions which are very much alive today and
which probably will be, as long as there is a human society. Think of the basically good, but weak men in any
position of authority today, and the peace in our time
which they have brought and continue to bring upon us.
Think of the insidious methods of evil men in positions
of authority and power, not only outside our boundaries
but close at hand as well. Think of the irreparable dam-
age done by those who act-- in the name of Christian
charity, but with no understanding in their hearts. The
question of whether and how to remove such men from
their influential positions is one which we most certainly have with us.

And lest I should give the impression that such questions are in the air merely and not being written about
by our own authors and playwrights, let me just cite two
works, one of the last century and one very much of our
own day, to remind you otherwise.

The same question is one of the central ones in
Moby Dick for example, made explicit when Starbuck
stands before Captain Ahab's bolted door and finds himself tormented by thoughts beyond his control. Shall the
warped man, though he is the repository of authority, in
a position made sacred by centuries of tradition, be allowed to carry the ship and its innocent crew to doom?

And is it not essentially the same question which is
central to the current very moving production of The
Caine Mutiny Court Martial, which presents the exon-
eration of the men who mutinied against Queeg, a captain
unfit to command, but which also reminds one sharply
that the victory over Queeg has its bitter side.

And finally, to bring the wheel full circle, is not
King Henry's problem, with which Shakespeare began
his career, much the same as Hamlet's, expressed by
the latter when he says:

What is a man,
If his chief good and market of his time
Be but to sleep and feed? A beast, no more.
Sure he that made us with such large discourse,
Looking before and after, gave us not
That capability and god-like reason
To fust in us unus'd. Now, whe'r it be
Bestial oblivion, or some craven scruple
Of thinking too precisely on the event,
A thought, which, quarter'd, hath but one part
      wisdom,
And ever three parts coward, I do not know
Why yet I live to say 'This thing 's to do';
Sith I have cause and will and strength and
      means
To do 't.

*   *   *

Rightly to be great
Is not to stir without great argument,
But greatly to find quarrel in a straw
When honour's at the stake.   How stand I then,
That have a father kill'd, a mother stain'd,
Excitements of my reason and my blood,
And let all sleep, while, to my shame, I see
The imminent death of Twenty thousand men,
That, for a fantasy and trick of fame,
Go to their graves like beds, fight for a plot
Whereon the numbers cannot try the cause,
Which is not tomb enough and continent to
      hide the slain?

RICHARDSON

I would urge upon you the thought that, imperfect as they are and certainly of their age, these plays, because of their importance in shedding light on the development of Shakespeare's career and, more important still, because of the relevant questions which they raise, are also for all time.

Eugene M. Waith

MACBETH: INTERPRETATION VERSUS ADAPTATION

"Confusion now hath made
his masterpiece!
Most sacrilegious murther
hath broke ope
The Lord's anointed temple,
and stole thence
The life o' th' building. "

--<u>Macbeth</u> (2.3.69-72)

March 3, 1954

James Thurber once wrote a story called "The Macbeth Murder Mystery." He describes meeting an American woman in the English Lake country who had had the misfortune to buy a paper-bound copy of <u>Macbeth</u>, thinking that it was a detective story. When she discovered her mistake her disgust was intense:

> "You can imagine how mad I was when I found it was Shakespeare. . . . I got real comfy in bed that night and all ready to read a good mystery story and here I had <u>The Tragedy of Macbeth</u>--a book for high-school students. Like Ivanhoe. . ."
> "Tell me," I said, "Did you read <u>Macbeth</u>?" I <u>had</u> to read it," she said. "There wasn't a scrap of anything else to read in the whole room." "Did you like it?" I asked. "No, I did not," she said decisively. "In the first place, I don't think for a moment that Macbeth did it. . . . I don't think the Macbeth woman was mixed up in it, either. You suspect them the most, of course, but those are the ones that are never guilty--or shouldn't be, anyway. . . . I've read that people never <u>have</u> figured out <u>Hamlet</u> so it isn't likely Shakespeare would have made <u>Macbeth</u> as simple as simple as it seems." I thought this over while I filled my pipe. "Who do you suspect?" I asked, suddenly. "Macduff," she said, promptly. . . . Do you know who discovered Duncan's body? . . . Macduff discovers it," she said, slipping into the historical present. "Then he comes running downstairs and shouts, 'Confusion has broke open

> the Lord's anointed temple' and 'Sacrile-
> gious murder has made his masterpiece'
> and on and on like that." The good lady
> tapped me on the knee. "All that stuff was
> <u>rehearsed</u>," she said. "You wouldn't say
> a lot of stuff like that, offhand, would you--
> if you had found a body? . . . You wouldn't!
> Unless you had practised it in advance.
> 'My God, there's a body in here!' is what
> an innocent man would say." She sat back
> with a confident glare.

This woman with her confident glare typifies the sort
of critic who feels free to rearrange the materials of the
work he is criticizing in any way that pleases him, ignoring this, imagining that. He may emerge with the theory
that Macduff is the murderer of Duncan or, as someone
once did, with the theory that Hamlet is a woman, ex-
plaining the hero's peculiar treatment of Ophelia and his
rather emotional friendship with Horatio. Now there is
no reason not to indulge in this sort of game, but it is
well to know what one is doing. This is not interpretation; it is adaptation. My topic this afternoon will be the
distinction between interpretation and adaptation as it
applies to <u>Macbeth</u>.

The problem is constantly encountered in the theater,
as Mr. McMullan's lecture clearly showed us. Every
production of a play rests on a conception of its meaning
and on the resulting choice to omit one thing or emphasize another. When the Mercury Theater in New York
put on a now famous <u>Julius Caesar</u>, Orson Welles presented Rome's dictator in the guise of Mussolini, with
the result that an American audience at the time of the
performance could scarcely feel that a valid principle of
order had been destroyed with Caesar. By this particular modernization the emphasis was so shifted that it became impossible to share Shakespeare's perception of
the tragic consequences of the assassination. Again,
there is no reason not to make a modern adaptation--it
may ultimately freshen our view of the play, as did this

production of Julius Caesar--but we must distinguish between this kind of treatment and interpretation.

The ideal production is one which accounts for every
feature of the play for which we have good textual author-
ity--one which brings out the underlying pattern to which
every detail relates. At such a performance of a Shakespearian tragedy we feel with increasing excitement, as
the play progresses, how each speech fits into place,
building toward the final recognition which completes the
meaning of the tragedy.

I don't pretend that I can give you the formula for the
ideal production of Macbeth nor that I can tell you in the
abstract where the boundary is that separates interpretation from adaptation. I shall take up a special case, where
the failure to understand certain conventions taken for
granted by Shakespeare's audience may lead us to over-
look the importance of the longest scene in Macbeth,
Act IV, Scene 3, which is rarely performed in its entire-
ty, and has been ignored by most critics. In modern
times L. C. Knights is almost alone in emphasizing its importance. No one has shown how some knowledge of
Shakespeare's age may point up the dramatic vitality
which is there. To skip over the scene is to lose some
brilliant theatrical effects and to risk misinterpreting
the play by undervaluing one of its major themes, the
theme of "sacrilegious murder."

Macbeth is not only a tragedy involving murder; it is
also a tragedy involving sacrilege. It is well known that
the murder of a king meant to an Elizabethan or Jacobean
the murder of a man whose office was divinely sanctioned
and who was therefore to some extent an agent of deity.
In fact James I, before whom Macbeth was performed,
wrote a little treatise for his son, the Prince of Wales,
in which he said, "Learn to know and love that God whom-
to ye have a double obligation; first for that he made you
a man, and next for that he made you a little God to sitte
on his throne, and rule over other men."

Shakespeare emphasizes the religious value of kingship at several points. The theme is introduced most
dramatically by Macduff in the passage misquoted by

WAITH

Thurber's friend:

> Confusion now hath made his masterpiece!
> Most sacrilegious murther hath broke ope
> The Lord's anointed temple, and stole thence
> The life o' th' building.

As the lady was well aware, this speech is not the most
usual sort of comment. It does, in a way, sound "rehearsed. " It is conceived in a style she would not recognize, though if she had been to an Elizabethan grammar
school, she would spot it as an example of the rhetorical
amplification of a point--an amplification which extends
our view momentarily to beyond the event. Among the
ideas exposed on this wider horizon sacrilege is prominent.

In Act III, Scene 6 come references to Macbeth's opposite number in England, Edward the Confessor--"most
pious Edward", the "holy king. " And at the end of the
play the religious note is sounded for one final time when
Malcolm promises to perform his new duties as King of
Scotland "by the grace of Grace. " But above all, this theme
is treated in the scene to which I have already referred,
Act IV, Scene 3, the longest scene in the play.

It would not occur to a contemporary writer present-
ing the tragedy of Macbeth to place this emphasis on the
religious value of kingship. One contemporary writer,
David Baird, has taken the events of Shakespeare's play
and, without altering them, has made them into a modern murder story called, The Thane of Cawdor. It is
instructive to compare the results. In Baird's novel the
story is told by the doctor; something of its quality may
be inferred from the opening: "The queen, my patient,
has now betrayed the terrible secret of the murder of
Duncan, " he begins. "This is no place to remain in for
one who has guessed that secret. . . . I was summoned
to the castle of Inverness to be in attendance on Lady
Macbeth not long before her husband had gone to the fight
against the rebels. Nothing could less suggest what was
to come than the beautiful castle of Macbeth with its pleas-

ant seat, its sweet and nimble air, where on every jetty, frieze, buttress and coign of vantage the martlet had its nest. " The occasional uncanny echo of Shakespeare merely accentuates the difference between the two ways of telling the same story. For this is the case of Lady Macbeth, the case of Macbeth, a clinical study of two criminal personalities. There is nothing of sacrilege here because divine law is beside the point.

Shakespeare's insistence upon the familiar Renaissance notions about the religious sanction of kingship, the religious dedication of the good ruler, is as necessary to his design as the witches, whom we must also accept on his terms. As they become powerful dramatic symbols of the evil forces tempting the hero, so the good ruler, God's vice-regent on earth, embodies the positive values which Macbeth turns against and tries to annihilate. By the use of such symbols Shakespeare constantly heightens our awareness of the ultimate implications of Macbeth's crime. He shows us that Macbeth's ambition is not only a threat to the entire kingdom of Scotland but a defiance of everything that makes him a man, with his special place in the divine scheme of things. Macbeth himself is keenly aware of these implications in the early part of the play:

> My thought, whose murther yet is but
> fantastical,
> Shakes so my single state of man
> That function is smother'd in surmise,
> And nothing is but what is not.

"My single state of man"--in that phrase macrocosm and microcosm, Scotland and Macbeth, are identified, and the further implication is made that Macbeth's humanity is threatened by the thought of his intended sacrilege, which will obscure all recognition of true value as it will overturn the government of Scotland. "Nothing is but what is not--Fair is foul and foul is fair--Confusion now hath made his masterpiece. "

Now the recognition of such relationships belongs, it

is true, to Shakespeare's age, not to ours. Yet it is possible to recover imaginatively something of the older view,
and it must be recovered if we are to achieve an interpretation, not an adaptation, of the play before us. The relationships I have just mentioned give the tragedy its stat-
ure, its cosmic grandeur. Remove them and you have
The Thane of Cawdor or "The Macbeth Murder Mystery."

Act IV, Scene 3 might be considered as a sort of
clue to the special world of this tragedy. But before I
discuss the scene, I had better remind you of what it contains, for it is unlikely that you have ever seen it performed, or thought very much about it. Few people do.
It is the scene in England, where Macduff, fleeing from
Scotland, meets Malcolm, the legitimate heir to the
throne. There are three sections, a long dialogue between Malcolm and Macduff, a short description of the
healing of the King's Evil by Edward the Confessor, and
a fairly long sequence in which Ross brings the news of
the Murder of Macduff's wife and children.

In the opening dialogue Malcolm behaves very strangely; he is suspicious that Macduff may be an agent sent by
Macbeth. For some time he holds Macduff at a distance,
answering him ambiguously, until Macduff, realizing that
he is suspected, starts to take his leave. During this
part of their talk Macduff twice breaks out in impassioned,
formal lament for the state of Scotland:

> Each new morn
> New widows howl, new orphans cry, new sorrows
> Strike heaven on the face, that it resounds
> As if it felt with Scotland and yell'd out
> Like syllable of dolor.

> Bleed, bleed, poor country!
> Great tyranny, lay thou thy basis sure,
> For goodness dare not check thee! Wear thou thy
> wrongs;
> The title is affeer'd.

As Macduff starts to go, Malcolm calls him back with as-

surances of good faith, but then begins to act even more
strangely. He says, well perhaps I could drive Macbeth
from the throne, but if I were king, Scotland would have
"more vices than before. "

> black Macbeth
> Will seem as pure as snow, and the poor state
> Esteem him as a lamb, being compar'd
> With my confineless harms.

> I grant him bloody,
> Luxurious, avaricious, false, deceitful,
> Sudden, malicious, smacking of every sin
> That has a name. But there's no bottom, none,
> In my voluptuousness: your wives, your daughters,
> Your matrons, and your maids, could not fill up
> The cistern of my lust, and my desire
> All continent impediments would o'erbear
> That did oppose my will. Better Macbeth
> Than such an one to reign.

Macduff is understandably shaken by this grim self-
portrait, but he says in effect, This is unfortunate, but
Scotland has "willing dames enough, " and I think we can
manage things discreetly to keep you satisfied and Scotland too.

But, says Malcolm, I am not only the world's most
energetic lecher; I am also such an insatiable miser that

> were I king,
> I should cut off the nobles for their lands,
> Desire his jewels and this other's house;
> And my more-having would be as a sauce
> To make me hunger more, that I should forge
> Quarrels unjust against the good and loyal,
> Destroying them for wealth.

This is more serious, says Macduff, but Scotland is a
rich country, and it all really belongs to you anyway, so
we can probably put up with your avarice, weighing it

against your virtues. But I have none, says Malcolm.

> The king-becoming graces,
> As justice, verity, temp'rance, stableness,
> Bounty, perseverance, mercy, lowliness,
> Devotion, patience, courage, fortitude,
> I have no relish of them, but abound
> In the division of each several crime,
> Acting it many ways. Nay, had I power, I should
> Pour the sweet milk of concord into hell,
> Uproar the universal peace, confound
> All unity on earth.

At this terrible catalogue Macduff's optimism finally
withers:

> These evils thou repeat'st upon thyself
> Hath banish'd me from Scotland. O my breast,
> Thy hope ends here!

Again he turns to go and again Malcolm detains him.
None of this is true, he says. I merely wanted to test
your sincerity. I am really unusually chaste, not in the
least covetous, and perfectly loyal. Macduff says truly

> Such welcome and unwelcome things at once
> 'Tis hard to reconcile.

And so indeed it has proved to most readers of the scene.
I have had to quote a great deal of the dialogue to show
you its quality and to emphasize what a strange performance it is. Most of it, like that earlier speech of Macduff's, sounds as if it had been "rehearsed." It must
have been one of the most unrewarding passages to Thurber's friend.

I shall pass much more rapidly over the remainder
of the scene. Before Macduff has recovered his compos-
ure a doctor appears whom Malcolm questions about King
Edward. The doctor explains that the king is about to
heal a throng of his ailing subjects by means of the divine

power of his touch. Malcolm tells Macduff that he has
often observed this miraculous power of King Edward's
and that some say the king's successors will inherit the
gift. In fact James I claimed to have done so, and therefore this little sequence has not seriously puzzled most
critics. Patent flattery, and not very subtle, they have
proclaimed, and have dismissed it. This it may be, but,
as I shall suggest, also more than this.

In the third part of the scene we are at last on familiar ground. Everyone remembers the way Ross first
pretends that all is well with Macduff's wife and children,
only to tell him a moment later that Macbeth has had
them murdered. The scene ends with Macduff's vow of
revenge and the plans of Malcolm and Macduff to lead an
army into Scotland with the aid of Edward the Confessor.

Here is the scene we are going to consider. It is
puzzling--the style is notably different from that of the
rest of the play--the relationship of the parts is not clear.
For these reasons the scene has had an odd history on
the stage, or rather, the odd part is that it has had almost no history on the stage. By pausing a moment over
this phenomenon one may catch a revealing glimpse of
the connection between the understanding of a play and
its performance.

Between the time Shakespeare wrote Macbeth and
the closing of the theaters in 1642 we may suppose that
this scene was acted, but we have no evidence. We know
only that some one, probably Middleton, had already
added to the witches' scenes even before the play was
printed in 1623. For about 20 years the theaters remained closed, and when they opened at the Restoration,
Macbeth was very popular. Pepys saw it several times
and commented especially on the excellence of the "divertisement," when he saw it in 1667. One might well wonder what he meant by divertisement. Apparently the
process of adding to the witches' scenes had continued
till there was what we would call a ballet at one or more
points. In 1674 Davenant's version of the play,very likely what Pepys saw, was printed. Here we can see exactly what was happening: there are several changes in the

dramatis personae, the spectacular witches' scenes are augmented and new ones are added; new music is introduced for the witches, and of course Shakespeare's native woodnotes wild are tamed and improved to harmonize with the concert of cultivated taste of the Restoration audiences. In short, this is an unabashed adaptation. From this time until 1744, Macbeth was seen only in this form.

In Davenant's adaptation the dialogue between Malcolm and Macduff is greatly reduced--the impersonation of an evil ruler is cut to about six lines; the description of Edward the Confessor is eliminated entirely. Only the third part is kept in something like its original form, but it becomes a scene by itself, separated from the first dialogue by one of Davenant's new scenes. Thus any structural unity of Shakespeare's scene is utterly destroyed.

In 1744 David Garrick announced that he would put on Macbeth as Shakespeare wrote it. So accustomed had the public become to the other version, whose authorship was unknown to many, that Garrick's announcement caused bewilderment in some quarters. Garrick's great rival, the actor Quin, is reported to have asked with rather pathetic naivete, "But isn't it Shakespeare that I have been acting?" And with all due respect to Garrick, who did much to rescue the play from the debauched state in which he found it, one may legitimately ask whether it was really Shakespeare he acted. He restored much of Shakespeare's language, but he retained some of Davenant's witch scenes and he added a dying speech for the hero (played by himself, of course), ending with the lines:

> my soul is clogg'd with blood --
> I cannot rise! I dare not ask for mercy --
> It is too late, hell drags me down; I sink,
> I sink -- Oh -- my soul is lost for ever!
> Oh!

Here, we must admit, the true Shakespearian flavor is somehow lacking.

As to Act IV, Scene 3, while Garrick restored its unity, eliminating Davenant's interpolation, he retained

112

MACBETH

Davenant's cuts. And so, surprisingly enough, did most
of the great actors who followed Garrick. In the middle
of the 19th century Macready and Phelps, two of the most
noted Macbeths, were known for their further restora-
tions of the original text, yet a Macready prompt-book
now in the Princeton library shows that he worked from
an edition which cut even some of what Garrick put back,
and Macready further cut the scene for himself. In a
Phelps prompt-book in the Yale library the cutting is
about the same as Garrick's.

In our own time, the edition of <u>Macbeth</u> as performed
at the imitation Globe Theater of the Chicago World's
Fair, cuts this scene from Malcolm's second speech to
the entrance of Ross. In a <u>Macbeth</u> arranged for little
theater production and put out only ten years ago everything before Ross's entrance is cut.

A few <u>critics</u> in our day have made a rather feeble
defense of the first part of the scene; scarcely any have
had a good word to say for the healing of the King's Evil:
"nothing to do with the progress of the drama, " says one;
"no interest whatever, " says another; "few would notice
or lament its absence, " says a third. Among these de-
spisers and dismissers I have already mentioned one exception, but like Canute, he has apparently not stopped
the rising waves.

If I were asked why, even amidst protestations of
ever closer allegiance to Shakespeare, more and more
of this scene has been nonchalantly handed to oblivion, I
believe I could answer very easily. It is clear enough
why Davenant didn't want it--it simply got in the way of
those singing witches and of the divertisement Pepys
enjoyed so much.

As to Garrick and his successors, their disinclina-
tion to Act IV, Scene 3 is more pertinent to the problem
we are considering. We must remember that Garrick is
famous as the actor who more than anyone else started
the movement toward realism in acting style; that Macready, 100 years later, was the most <u>natural</u> Macbeth
up to that time and that this naturalness was his claim to
fame. If we then think of the rhetorical speeches of Mac-

duff and the highly contrived posing of Malcolm, it is easy
to see why actors in an increasingly realistic theater have
tended to skip this part of the play. Fanny Kemble made
a comment about Macready which may have been malicious
but may also have been true. She said his "natural" way
of saying the lines was due purely to his inability to speak
blank verse, a difficulty under which many contemporary
actors of Shakespeare also labor. Surely the failure to
deal properly with the artifice of blank verse is intimately related to an unwillingness to attempt this scene.

I should say, then, that the scene had been the victim
of two tendencies, one toward spectacle and one toward
realism. As Mr. McMullan's lecture made clear, these
two, different as they are, have often gone hand in hand.
In the long run the demands of realism have probably been
the more devastating, for they have sought nothing less
than the elimination of whatever is not psychologically
credible and whatever does not contribute immediately to
the portrayal of character, the analysis of motive, or the
progress of events toward the hero's fall. Such demands
point the way toward Thurber's Lady of the Lake Country
--a witch whom I should like to remove from the play.
For the spell of psychological realism results in an adaptation just as surely as does the lure of spectacle.

Act IV, Scene 3 is in a different key from most of the
other parts of the play. For that very reason its restate-
ment and expansion of certain themes of the tragedy are
the more striking. The Jacobean audience, one may assume, was moved by this modulation and had no desire
to skip over it, as the adapters do, nor to attempt to
transpose the action back into the main key of the play.
Presumably its very individuality of style recommended
it. The spectator who had been to grammar school (and
you will recall from Mr. Harding's lecture how wide
spread this education was) might well relish this scene,
because he had been trained from his youth to admire elo-
quence and to appreciate the various devices of rhetoric
which appear in the dialogue here. Macduff is given
some very eloquent speeches: "Each new morn / New
widows howl, new orphans cry . . ." "Bleed, bleed, poor

country!'" "O Scotland, Scotland . . . O nation miserable!
/ With an untitled tyrant bloody sceptred. " And Malcolm,
as we have seen, is given extended passages in which he
must assume a character unlike his own. Any graduate
of a grammar school would recognize in this procedure a
special use of an exercise with which he was very familiar. For he had been obliged to learn the art of debate
and in learning it he had had to pretend to be some historical or fictitious character, faced by some sensationally
complicated situation. He had then had to devise and de-
liver a speech defending his conduct. He took the part of
the man who executed Cicero on Antony's orders or of a
father demanding that his son be put to death for filial
ingratitude. This same student might then have had to
turn around and present the case against Cicero's execu-
tioner and against the father, making monsters of cruel-
ty out of the characters he had just assumed. Something
like this is familiar enough to us in the form of legal
training, but it no longer enters into our standard training in composition as it did in the Renaissance.

Our Jacobean spectator, then, could enjoy the dialogue of Malcolm and Macduff as a kind of intellectual
game--a debate in which these like-minded people had
been assigned opposite sides. The preposterous contrast
between the true and the assumed merely makes the game
more fascinating to watch. Of course the spectator was
aware that it was not purely a game--that Malcolm was
testing Macduff, as the histories recorded--but the
Jacobean was not so distracted as we are apt to be by
the question of the probability of such a scene. If he
was familiar with Holinshed's account of the meeting,
he knew that Shakespeare, instead of making it seem
more likely, had heightened its improbabilities at every
turn.

The improbability could be accepted as part of a
recognized rhetorical convention, and it could be justified on other grounds as well. John Masefield makes
the acute observation that this scene gives the two men
a remarkable opportunity for acting, and that Shakespeare may have wished to repeat the histrionic success

of his popular scene in <u>Julius Caesar</u>, where Brutus and
Cassius quarrel only to make friends once more. If we
wish to find out what Malcolm and Macduff might have done
with their debate, we may again turn to the books on rhetoric, for the acting techniques of the day grew out of the
same sort of training as that which underlies the composition of the scene. In some of these books can be seen copious illustrations of what I might call "hand-signals" to
express each emotion. Some were sweeping and extrava-
gant, like those we now associate with old-fashioned elo-
cution; others were of an extraordinary refinement. For
example, the right hand raised with only the little finger
extended was to accompany the explanation of some very
subtle point. But if all the fingers of this hand were extended except for the fourth finger, that meant, "I touch
lightly upon . . ." It is clear that the manner of speaking
on the stage as on the rostrum was highly stylized by our
realistic standards. And acting style differed from other
public speaking only in being more extreme. Returning
to our scene, we shall find that the text indicates one gesture required, when Malcolm tells Macduff not to pull his
hat upon his brows, as he has apparently done upon hearing the news of his wife's murder. This quaint way of
expressing grief seems to have had some connection with
actual behavior, for there are drawings of melancholy
men with hats almost over their eyes. It is well to remember too that the courtesy books, while condemning
affectation, encouraged the cultivation of suitable gestures
to express the speaker's emotions, even in ordinary con-
versation. Hence, the style of acting was not a flat contradiction of what was familiar, but nevertheless a notable
formalization, recognized as proper in the sphere of ora-
tory or the theater. We may imagine that Malcolm and
Macduff conveyed their various emotions by a variety of
nicely calculated formal gestures.

In parentheses let me suggest that the acting of this
scene today should aim not a precise historical recrea-
tion of 17th century gesture, which might reduce the audience to helpless laughter. It should rather aim at a com-
parable degree of formalization--at what will be recog-

nized as a different key.

The scene under discussion might, then, be justified in part as providing a splendid opportunity for a virtuoso display of a gamut of emotions. Malcolm is seen first as sad and suspicious--next as a saturnine tyrant--then suddenly as a noble prince and loyal friend--finally as a staunch comforter. Macduff must display first the courage of despair, then doubt, then a desperate optimism in the face of Malcolm's alarming self-portrait, then utter despair, followed by confusion, grief, anger, and finally the courage of hope. At each point the emotions of the one character are nicely set off by the emotions of the other. The original acting technique undoubtedly heightened the impression of formal contrast.

But the scene is also valuable in other ways. The Jacobean spectator would have sensed immediately what it requires a little effort for us to see, that Malcolm's persona, or mask, makes possible a standard method of advancing an argument--the development by contraries, or contentio, as it was called. The theme developed in this way is the divine character of the ideal ruler--a theme closely related to the testing of Macduff, but at the same time on a different level, that of abstract thought. So that as we enjoy the technical brilliance of the contrasting attitudes,--the suddenly shifting emotions, and as we watch Malcolm testing the sincerity of Macduff in this highly contrived fashion, we also see beyond the characters of the tragedy to an idea which dramatically unfolds as the scene progresses.

We are given first a striking picture of the consequences of misrule--a Scotland where "each new morn new widows howl, new orphans cry"--a country whose social structure is being violently destroyed. As the author of this disturbance, Macbeth is referred to as tyrant, treacherous, black, devilish--but Malcolm's persona creates for us an imaginary figure which is even worse--an abstract of the qualities of the evil ruler. The attributes of this figure are taken up one by one to be subjected to Macduff's comment: Lechery, Avarice, finally a superhuman principle of disruption, like Satan himself:

> Nay, had I power, I should
> Pour the sweet milk of concord into hell,
> Uproar the universal peace, confound
> All unity on earth.

This is, for one thing, a rhetorical elaboration of the term "devil" applied to Macbeth; but it is more than this: it is a substantial projection of Macbeth's worst potentialities. It is, in other words, the ideal evil latent in him. Such implications are reinforced by the connection we must make between this vision of chaos and the earlier statement of Macduff: "Confusion now hath made his masterpiece." On the level of abstraction to which the rhetoric leads us these two speeches meet.

The naked logic of Malcolm's portrayal of the evil ruler is emphasized by the exact patterning of contrasts. Early in the scene Macbeth as an "angry god" is contrasted to Malcolm as a "weak, poor innocent lamb." When Malcolm assumes his mask,

> black Macbeth
> Will seem as pure as snow, and the poor
> state
> Esteem him as a lamb . . .

In the imagery the white lamb sets off the darkness of the angry god as, in the strategy of the dialogue, Malcolm and Macduff constantly set off each other.

Another exact contrast appears when the list of Macbeth's qualities ("I grant him bloody, / Luxurious, avaricious, etc.") is balanced by the list of the "king-becoming graces" ("As justice, verity, temp'rance . . . bounty, etc.") Finally, when Malcolm removes his mask, he sets forth a formal enumeration of his true qualities as a further contrast to those he temporarily assumed.

By these dialectical means the depiction of the evil ruler has been carried to the point of showing him as archetypal evil--Satan; and to this figure has been op-

posed the symbol of the innocent lamb, a list of qualities
admirable in a king, and the portrayal of the true Malcolm
as a virtuous man. If we realize that the argument has
reached this point as we come to the end of the dialogue
between Malcolm and Macduff, the sequence of the King's
Evil will no longer seem irrelevant:

> at his touch,
> Such sanctity hath heaven given his hand,
> They presently amend.

> How he solicits heaven,
> Himself best knows; but strangely-visited
> people,
> All swolne and ulcerous, pitiful to the eye,
> The mere despair of surgery, he cures,
> Hanging a golden stamp about their necks,
> Put on with holy prayers;
> With this strange virtue
> He hath a heavenly gift of prophecy,
> And sundry blessings hang about his throne
> That speak him full of grace.

Here at last is the proper contrast to Malcolm's impersonation of the evil ruler. To the disruptive Satan is
opposed a king with the supernatural powers of healing
and restoring. To be sure, this is a description of a
real king, Edward the Confessor, but the portrait is
clearly larger than life size. King Edward never appears
on the stage. He remains a force behind Malcolm, an
ideal of the good ruler, God's vice-regent, a "little god, "
almost a principle of good rule. It is this principle that
Macbeth assaulted when his sacrilegious murther broke
ope the Lord's anointed temple. Hence the description
of Edward the Confessor, by making clear what con-
structive values are threatened by Macbeth, comple-
ments the earlier depiction of him as the murderer of
sleep, nature's great restorative, and the disrupter of
the banquet, the ceremony which should symbolize political stability.

WAITH

The third section of this scene, the portion in which
Macduff hears from Ross of the murder of his children,
is again characterized by artful rhetoric. Though his
message concerns Macduff most immediately and most
tragically, Ross begins with a general statement of the
woes of Scotland which echoes Macduff's first speech.
When directly questioned by Macduff, he answers ambiguously, and while seeming to say that Macduff's family
is well, hints that something dire has befallen them. The
most significant result of this curious sparring is his re-
ply when Macduff asks whether his news concerns the
general cause or the personal grief of some individual.
Ross says:

> No mind that's honest
> But in it shares some woe, though the main
>   part
> Pertains to you alone.

Macduff's grief is Scotland's grief. Once again the function of the rhetorical presentation, beyond the heighten-
ing of dramatic suspense, is to emphasize the general
meaning of a particular situation.

When the news is finally given, we are prepared by
all that has come before to see the murder of Macduff's
wife and children as the logical outcome of the sacrilegious murder which gave Macbeth the throne. And Macduff is established by his reaction to the news as the
ideal human agent of the restorative powers seen at their
highest in the almost divine Edward. Macduff qualifies
for this role by the intensity of his moral concern not
only with Macbeth's evil but with his own in leaving his
family unguarded:

> Not for their own demerits, but for mine,
> Fell slaughter on their souls.

This is a very different self-accusation from Malcolm's
earlier in the scene. Where that was assumed, this is
a sincere recognition of moral responsibility, showing

120

that Macduff possesses what Macbeth has annihilated in himself.

The testing of Macduff, begun in the first part of the scene has gone far beyond the testing of his political af- filiation: it has tested him by a standard of absolute good. Macduff is not a saint, like Edward, and he is more human than Malcolm, who appears in this scene as a sort of mediator between the worlds of the ideal and the actual. Malcolm must organize the forces of good, but he is not himself the agent to deal with Macbeth. The strategy of the scene is such that the appealing humanity of Macduff is set off against the more remote nobility of Malcolm, while behind them both is the glorious but shadowy figure of Edward the Confessor. It is Macduff who will translate into heroic action the conflict between good and evil which has been presented in dialectical form. The full range of that conflict is felt in his mov- ing words:

> Front to front
> Bring thou this fiend of Scotland and myself;
> Within my sword's length set him; if he scape,
> Heaven forgive him too!

This is the logical culmination of a scene which has, so to speak, reviewed the nature of Macbeth's crime, pushing our perceptions beyond the pale of the everyday world. It is dramatically right that when the enormity of the evil has been made almost unbearably clear, a champion should be found to ride into battle. As Mal- colm says, "the powers above / Put on their instru- ments. "

The ideal production of the <u>Macbeth</u> which appeared in the Shakespeare Folio of 1623, then, will not be based on an arbitrary selection of what most obviously appeals to the 20th century, but will be faithful to the whole de- sign of the play as we have it. It will be put on with mod- ern devices of lighting and stage setting, but in such a way as to provide the modern equivalents of the 17th cen- tury devices, just as the modern editor usually intro-

duces modern punctuation which is equivalent to the Elizabethan but not identical with it.   In the ideal production
of <u>Macbeth</u> Act IV, Scene 3 will take its place as an in-
tegral part of a tightly organized artistic entity.   If properly done, in a style more formal than that of the rest of
the play, we shall find this scene an absorbing and at
times very moving preparation for the final defeat of the
man who dared do more than becomes a man--of the hero
who lacked only the power to

> Uproar the universal peace, confound
> All unity on earth.

Norman Holmes Pearson

ANTONY AND CLEOPATRA

> "Yet, if I knew
> What hoop should hold us
>   stanch, from edge to edge
> O' the world I would pursue
>   it. "
>
> --<u>Antony and Cleopatra</u> (2.2)

March 10, 1954

There is a little game with which every one, sooner or later, diverts himself. On occasion it takes the form simply of choosing one's favorite play by Shakespeare; more ambitiously, of naming the best play. The two need not be the same, of course, though it is pleasanter to think so. Diversity of opinion is a characteristic of the immense audience for Shakespeare's plays, which has grown from that first Elizabethan audience which Mr. Harding described in his lecture. Perhaps it is this multiplicity of preference which accounts for the immensity of the audience; certainly it is the wealth of possible choice which accounts for the fact that when we think of Shakespeare, even the most partisan thinks of the whole canon and not a single play. Yet I suspect I know why I have been asked to talk about <u>Antony and Cleopatra</u>. I once committed myself to it, and such loyalty demands a certain definition. My memory goes back to a morning in New York, some years ago now, when Mr. W. H. Auden and I came to that point in the making of an anthology when we had to choose the play by Shakespeare with which to represent the culmination of verse drama in the Elizabethan age. Being concerned as I am, at this moment, with a drama as the subject of my talk, my mind may dramatize my memory. But I remember our standing across the room from one another, as though the distance between us would parry the conflict of opinions. We hesitated, but when our mouths opened they opened together, and simultaneously we had chosen <u>Antony and Cleopatra</u>.

But not every one has agreed about Shakespeare's

achievement. Mr. C. B. Young, in a note on "The Stage
History of Antony and Cleopatra, " has reminded us of a
long period of public indifference to it. From Shakespeare's time, "down to the middle of the nineteenth century, " he says, "all but total neglect seems to have overcome the play. Only with Phelps's revival in 1849 (the
same Phelps, by the way, whom Mr. Waith discussed in
relation to Macbeth) did the theatrical world begin to take
an interest in it. ... " So much for a prolonged eclipse,
when the curtain was seldom raised on Antony and Cleopatra. In the world of critical taste, we remember Sir
Walter Scott's admiration for Dryden's version, All For
Love, and his unequivocal preference for "the plan of
Dryden's play ... to that of Shakespeare in point of co-
herence, unity, and simplicity. " Scott's praise extended
to "the beauty of (Dryden's) language and imagery, which
is flowery, " he says, "without diffuseness, and rapturous
without hyperbole. I fear," he went on, "that Shakespeare
cannot be exculpated from the latter fault; yet I am sensible, it is by sifting his beauties from his conceits that
his imitator has been enabled to excel him. " So much
for Scott and the lingering reasoning of the eighteenth
century.

The objections have continued. Almost at the same
moment, in 1947, when I expressed what I can only call
my pledge to Antony and Cleopatra, I read a review in
the New York World-Telegram of Katherine Cornell's
spectacular appearance in the play. The reviewer said:

> (She)has done everything physically possible
> to make her presentation of Shakespeare's An-
> tony and Cleopatra a great production. ... It is
> the Bard himself who lets her down, for the play
> remains a monumental bore. It calls for inex-
> plicable pageantry and inundates the personal
> story beneath an everlasting tangle of warring
> politics. The two main proponents are intro-
> duced as cases of wilful arrested development.
> They have neither majesty nor stature in what
> they do, and nothing said about them keeps their

love from seeming self indulgent and sordid.
It is difficult to care what happens to them.
They only achieve the grandeur history suggests, when they begin to lose everything.
The play has magnificent disdain for classic
unities. It moves all around the eastern Med-
iterranean, picking up meetings in Rome,
battles in Syria and adulteries in Egypt. This
multitude of scenes has been adroitly cut, but
the condensation does not cure the play's ver-
boseness.

So much for that.

A few weeks ago I asked a friend what he considered
the chief difficulty of the play. His thoughtful answer
was in terms of the audience. Shakespeare, he said, requires much more of us, and in a different way, from
what our usual situation is in regard to the characters of
a dramatic work in the theatre. For we normally judge
characters, whether in a play or in life, by their actions;
here we are asked to assess them finally by their words.
We are not used to depending so much on words when we
hear them spoken. He was right. Antony and Cleopatra
is a play on words, as well as a play made from them.
The action revolves about words and their justness. We
can watch the action of Antony and Cleopatra with attention, but we must hear and remember with concentration
the words which accompany the action. Only as these
spoken words remain firmly with us, fixed but lively in
our consciousness, can we fully see the conflict between
what the players say and what they do, and feel the progress of the drama through a series of tensions toward
the final apocalyptic congruence.

The life as well as the particular quality of Antony
and Cleopatra come from this interplay. The initial dis-
parity of action and statement on the part of the two chief
characters makes the validity of their first declarations
seem absurd although beautiful, mere lovers' exaggerations, pure hyperbole of the sort to which Scott's reasoning objects. On the other hand, it is the suitability of

their irresponsible deeds to Philo's opening and choragic disapproval of them, which makes the quasi-anonymous Philo seem, at the beginning, the proper rhetorician and the impartial judge. From this conflict of opening impressions, the progress of the play stems; and it continues in the achievement of definitions, establishing some and destroying others, until at the end we understand in triumphant awareness, parallel to a tragic awareness though mollified, what neither we nor the chorus nor Antony and Cleopatra themselves could, at the opening, fully grasp in the clarification of character and diction.

If in practise I prefer to read Antony and Cleopatra rather than see it performed on the stage, it is because the process of understanding is simplified on the printed page. The words which I can thus see with concentration, take precedence over the action, which I can only fancy. I can linger over the printed words, delaying the action until I have absorbed the words, as I linger over the verbal counters of a poem. Where words become supreme in this way, almost at the expense of action, we approach the realm of the closet drama rather than the theatre. It would be inept to consider Antony and Cleopatra simply as a poem rather than a play, but in this instance we are close to that thin line which divides poetic drama from a dramatic poem. Certainly the intensely, almost metaphysically contrived verbal texture of Antony and Cleopatra--Shakespeare's sense of words which waver in definition and must be filled with significance established within the play itself--brings the manner of this drama close to the verbal excitement which is the stimulant of much of our contemporary concern with poetry. It is no wonder that Coleridge admired this particular work so much.

But perhaps there is something to be said, after all, for Dryden as man of the theatre. He made no such demands, in his version, as Shakespeare does, either on actors or audience. What the theatre uniquely gives, of course, is visible action as a mode of definition and a way towards understanding. That which is most theatrical is apt to be least wordy. Words are usually subordinate in the theatre to movement on the stage. That is one reason, for example, why there is no play by Eugene O'Neill which is not more interesting when staged than read. For O'Neill knew the ways of the theatre better than he knew the ways of language. Dryden knew language, but he simplified its use in verse. Action in his play becomes dominant in a straight though impassioned line; verse follows it. Dryden's play is first-class theatre and good poetry. It is only when we compare it, as an absolute literary achievement, to Shakespeare's ironic and ultimately triumphant interinvolvement of words with action, that All For Love diminishes in appeal and we can understand what makes Antony and Cleopatra so terrifying to produce and so overwhelmingly a display of the absolute limits of drama.

Both Shakespeare and Dryden, in any event, could work with material that was familiar. Not needing to invent, Shakespeare could interpret. Perhaps Antony and Cleopatra, as a play, would have been more difficult for his Elizabethan imagination to push towards the limits of drama, if its principal characters were not already at home in the theatre and in the fancy of the audience. The Countess of Pembroke had written in verse The Tragedy of Antony in 1592; Samuel Daniel, her protege, had done The Tragedy of Cleopatra as a companion in 1594. Shakespeare seems to have known the latter, when, about 1607, he wrote his own play. Some phrases from Daniel's abundance Shakespeare gallantly took over. But Cleopatra had her own niche anyhow. She lived in the general imagination as a dark angel, a tanned Helen of the Nile. Chaucer and Lydgate knew her; a good woman and a pitiable one. Shakespeare, however, could find her entertainment closer to his time. (And I ought to explain that many of these possible introductions to her have been shown me by Mr. Walter King, of the English Department at Yale.) "The beauty and the good grace of Cleopatra" were in Painter's Palace of Pleasure; her "lovely looks" in Gascoigne's Sundry Flowers--"but brown I dare be bold she was," he says. In A Petite Palace of Pettie His Pleasure, Cleopatra was "that black Egyptian," but

still her "courtesy" was "incomparable." Nashe brought
her forth, time upon time again; as Florio did, and
Greene. Elyot knew her in his Book of the Governor, and
Lyly in his Euphues. She lived as a familiar to the age.

She was the stuff of drama, so was Antony. Shakespeare worked with them for his play, much as Mr. Richardson has shown him working with the early histories;
and Antony and Cleopatra were history of course. Plu-
tarch had seen to that, and North had helped. Antony and
Cleopatra had the dignity which history gives; they filled
the interest curiosity can breed. Their scope extended
through the world; they made the costumed pageantry of
a masque. And they held tragedy: they fell. This was
enough to make a play of.

Yet the play we have, seems so purely to come out
of Shakespeare himself, that the theme must have held a
particular interest and appeal for him, quite apart from
what would "go" on the stage, and make that kind of production which Mr. McMullan so well explains and equally
well adapts. Inherently, for Shakespeare, there was the
"problem"--to put the word in quotes--to make the drama
felt by him. Why should an Antony have done these things?
Was Cleopatra worthy of the sacrifice? What was the significance of love, or love like theirs?

Love was ubiquitous to Shakespeare as a theme. But
especially there had been the sonnets, and the dark lady.
There was Romeo and Juliet, and several kinds of love in
it. "Cleopatra ('s) a gypsy," he had Mercutio say, com-
paring Romeo's Juliet to the tawny queen. But here, in
1607, is the Shakespeare who is middle-aged, describing
middle-age, when Cleopatra reappears to him. Shakespeare was 43, and Antony was 43, by history, when this
play takes place. I do not say that Antony was Shakespeare, only that the Bard had sympathy; and sympathy
is good for drama as for life. It is good for criticism,
too.

But what of the nature of the material of his play.
This was a regal scene, of Egypt and of Rome, which
Shakespeare had, and had to use, as background. Others
than Shakespeare knew the rich demands of style. They

dressed their imagery to suit the splendor too. Selden,
for example, later in the century, in Dryden's time, tried
out the play in rhyme. He had Octavia die, and had Maecenas eloquently say of her:

> From out the Crystal Palace of her breast,
> Her clearer soul is gone to endless rest.
> What time, what reason can my loss digest.

But despite the unhappy comparison of these lines with
Charmion's tribute to the dying Cleopatra, and even
though the Great Exhibition of 1851 now comes inevitably
between us and the swelling beauty of this Crystal Palace
of Octavia's Roman breast, it is evident that the figures
of speech are less than rhetorically digested into the texture of Selden's verse, quite apart from any other diges-
tive problems Maecenas's grief might have met. It is
Shakespeare's extraordinary power that makes his own
figures of speech dramatically active and organic rather
than merely ornamental or tasty. There is purple in the
passages of the play, but it is imperial and not patch.
Even Enobarbus's supreme description of Cleopatra, as
she approaches on the Cydnus, is not pure display but
tactics of language. For Antony and Cleopatra is a drama
of persuasion, an exercise in rhetoric which will explain
and justify the values which a Roman world ignores.

"I will tell you, " Enobarbus says, but not simply to
Agrippa and Maecenas who are with him in his return to
a Roman world. Enobarbus speaks also as though to
Caesar and to Lepidus who do not hear. He speaks to
Pompey, too; for none of these Romans can understand
what drew the "demi-Atlas of the world" to Egypt. Egypt
and Cleopatra are beyond their experience. Enobarbus,
reaching for the limits of sensory verse, tries to create
experience as a magnet for these two who stand as sur-
rogate for all the rest.

Can't you sense it! he seems to say. Listen to me!
It's this way! For poetry describes the quality of things;
and Cleopatra's quality is what Enobarbus grasps, in
words that spring forth like a vision not before beheld by

us, for we have seen too little of her;--until now, that is,
since Enobarbus also speaks to us. Sight, sound, smell,
touch bombard us; and we learn from these what reason
will not tell but "flower-soft hands" can give. "O, rare
for Antony!" Agrippa says, when Enobarbus finishes his
first verse paragraph. Agrippa thinks, as we have thought,
of Antony imperially apart from us, and Cleopatra wrought
for him alone. But when the verse goes on, and "a strange
invisible perfume hits the sense of the adjacent wharfs,"
Agrippa cries out this time, "Rare Egyptian!" His ex-
clamation shifts its referent. Antony is forgotten. Agrippa thinks now only of the queen, for she has conquered
him in verse, and he runs "to gaze on Cleopatra too." We
run on with him and the crowd. We have begun to share
with Antony.

Such is the persuasion of this single little scene within the play, but it works more. It helps define such early
words as these, which Cleopatra spoke to Antony:

> Eternity was in our lips and eyes,
> Bliss in our brows bent; none our parts so poor
> But was a race of heaven. They are so still...

From the first lines of the play, this effort, through language and feeling, to break through the limits of reason
to that which cannot be "reckon'd", provides the essential
dramatic strain.

> Cleo. I'll set a bourn how far to be belov'd.
> Ant.   Then must thou needs find out new
>   heaven, new earth.

It is such a glimpse of heaven that Enobarbus gives, an
apotheosis that lifts Cleopatra up from the rank of queen
to that of goddess of Love and finally to an estate of pure
sense. Thus, none their "parts so poor" but can become
a race (that is, a root) of heaven. More definition is still
needed before Cleopatra is again for Cydnus, but Enobarbus has added something to her realization, and the words
of the play have progressed in their special manner.

ANTONY AND CLEOPATRA

Enobarbus's description of Cleopatra's welcome at Cydnus prepares us also to learn something about the character of Caesar. That is, if Enobarbus's lines are, as they should be, still fresh in mind when we read Caesar's analagous description of the "ideal" approach of his sister, Octavia, to Rome:

Caes: Sister: The wife of Antony
        Should have an army for an usher, and
        The neighs of horse to tell of her approach,
        Long ere she did appear. The trees by the way
        Should have borne men, and expectation fainted,
        Longing for what it had not. Nay, the dust
        Should have ascended to the roof of Heaven,
        Raised by your populous troops. But you are
                come
        A market-maid to Rome, and have prevented
        The ostentation of our love; which left unshown
        Is often left unlov'd. We should have met you
        By sea, and land, supplying every stage
        With an augmented greeting.

What sort of expectation faints? One, choked by the dust the horses raised, while "longing" for fresh air "it had not?" Not this, of course, but one to be overcome by a display of pomp or expectation of it. And what is that which "left unshown is often left unlov'd"? It is the "ostentation" of a brother's love, made a show of, exhibited through troops, and not by heart-felt tropes. Is this a brother's love? Will "market-maid" prove in the end to be so foul an epithet, when we find Cleopatra as "the maid that milks and does the meanest chares, "--"a lass unparallel'd"? Octavius stays aloof; he does not share, at best he but bestows. Only what's rank, not ripeness, counts for him.

It is not simply that Caesar's diction differs from that of Enobarbus. Caesar's words should not have been the same as Enobarbus's. A brother's love is different, but it should be love. We know Octavius Caesar through the words he chooses. And though these words are rea-

sonable, he is not capable of that personal emotion which
informs words as poetry, any more than he is capable of
such felt love for his sister as would have prevented his
attempts to hoop the world together through the cold for-
mality of Octavia's Roman marriage to Antony. Caesar
is defined for us, not by any direct statements about his
character--or at least by comparatively few of them--
but dramatically: partly by contrast of his words and
deeds, and also by contrast of his words with those which
others speak: Enobarbus in this case, and Antony almost
everywhere. Caesar's lines are flat. It is not Shakespeare's lack, but Caesar's, in them.

No wonder then that Antony can scorn this beardless
boy of 23, who had not wived and could not love, was
passionless, had never singly fought in combat but had
"worded" men and made his way by tricks of conscience.
Caesar spoke eloquently of honor, friendship, unity and
love, but never knew each as a fact. So Lepidus, too,
slung words about, flabby, with no core in them. This
Pompey understood:

> Caesar gets money where
> He loses hearts; Lepidus flatters both,
> Of both is flattered; but he neither loves,
> Nor either cares for him.

It is this absence of felt love, even the denial of the capacity for love, which marks the world and the language
of the world which Caesar makes.

More than the empire split in bits after the death of
Julius Caesar by the swords. Man himself divides,
matching the splinters. Man's personal nature is no
longer whole, when as a citizen his allegiance must be
pledged either to one half or the other of the world.
Nothing remains between the poles. One can begin to
understand Antony and Cleopatra better, as a play, if,
as Professor Bethel and others have shown us, we see
the ultimate opposition between Rome and Egypt not simply as a political struggle for power, but as a conflict
between two ways of life expressed by the extremes.

ANTONY AND CLEOPATRA

Between them Antony is pulled. Roman values of duty are opposed to Egyptian values of pleasure; reason against intuition; mind against the senses; shrewdness against idealism; and prudence against daring. In a world which is a whole, these values need not be in conflict, for a whole world at peace had contained both Rome and Egypt too. Each way of life is a part of that reduced facsimile of the world which man himself becomes. But let man place too great an emphasis upon one set of values in himself: this set will crowd the other out, as it itself expands in opportunity. Make one extreme: its adversary too becomes extreme, and there are nothing but extremes to choose from.

This was what Rome had done, and Caesar was its icon. Honor became debased. At best it was a word without a soul, though highly polished by much use. Caesar had learned to tongue it late in its career in Roman talk; Antony had learned it young, and mourned its gradual loss of quality. Antony was a man. What had been starved by Roman ways he hungered for. Deprive a man of food for years, and he will gorge when once he has the chance. Antony craved more than power, and could not find the things he sought in Rome.

If hunger is a common urge, and shared by men alike, the goals of hunger must, then, be defined and understood. Caesar, for example, was young and hungered. Caesar hungered for power; but since the world was already conquered, he could only, as Antony would not, prey upon friends. Or rather, Caesar did not feel these people as his friends; nor think of _honor_ save as it became a useful word to flaunt; or _order_ save as an excuse for seizing power, to be achieved by foment of discord. Nothing stood in his way: not friendship, which is based on love; nor honor, which depends on loyalty. These qualities he lacked, and when he used the words, he tricked with them to cover up the motive underneath. His deeds belied his words, --if when we think of deeds we can forget his dignity of movement on the stage, his toga'd wrap of hollow, polished words, remembering Caesar as he is when he fights Pompey,

or tricks Lepidus, or knowingly slights Antony, and
breaks the spirit of his word, as others understood the
meaning from his speech, and only later knew it was not
so from what he did.

For Antony the usual tokens of aspiration were a-
chieved. A man has fame, is conqueror, a triumvir,
had done the things he does so well that repetition has
no meaning any more. And these are not enough: something is lacking, and he is not whole. Antony felt only
partial so he plunged, splashing the past in quest of
something more:

> Let Rome in Tiber melt, and the wide arch
> Of the rang'd empire fall! Here is my space.
> Kingdoms are clay; our dungy earth alike
> Feeds beast as man; the <u>nobleness of life</u>
> Is to do this; when such a mutual pair
> (Embracing)
> And such a twain can do't, in which I bind,
> On pain of punishment, the world to weet
> We stand up peerless.

Possibly Antony could only recognize and could not
really define the urge which drove him toward Egypt,
away from Rome, away from Fulvia and his Roman marriage to her, as later it would send him off from Caesar
and Octavia. This was a kind of spiritual and physical
restlessness such as a long-starved middle age can feel,
when nothing man has won has satisfied. This was the
straining, through the surge of feeling and language, to
break the limits of reason--to repeat an observation
made apropos of Enobarbus's and Cleopatra's speech.
Antony now felt the "nobleness of life" and could make
poetry of it. He had his intimations of the "heaven" and
the "eternity" which Cleopatra felt. For Antony, his
mind too clouded o'er with Roman thought, Egypt seemed clothed in a celestial light. "And I again am strong"
he might have said, had Antony been born in Wordsworth's time. I am not trying to make the Nile Delta
into the Lake Country of the Roman world, but their

recreational benefits to knowledge through the senses
have something romantically in common all the same.
Antony had met Egypt on her burnished barge, and one
might say of him:

> The Rainbow comes and goes,
> And lovely is the Rose...

And to quote further from Wordsworth (was his "Ode:
Intimations of Immortality" unconsciously commenting
on Cydnus, and preparing for the defeat of Sir Walter
Scott and Scott's views?):

> And all the earth is gay;
>   Land and sea
> Give themselves up to jollity,
>   And with the heart of May
> Doth every beast keep holiday;--
>   Thou Child of Joy,
> Shout round me, let me hear thy shouts,
>   thou happy Triumvir!

Or was it "thou happy shepherd-boy" that Wordsworth
wrote to keep the rhyme? Antony now happy at Cydnus
needed a new definition. Wordsworth may have been
right in reducing Antony's social status.

Though the way to knowledge for the romantics is
through the senses rather than through the reason,
Wordsworth was less willing to place such emphasis on
love as a *vade mecum* as Shakespeare did; at least when
Wordsworth recollected Annette in tranquility. The
mere sight of the barge would have been enough for
Wordsworth's shepherd-boy, and Wordsworth would not
have approved of the Roman-boy's hunger for understanding when, "barber'd ten times o'er," he went to
feast with Cleopatra. Wordsworth's was a more limit-
edly individual redemption, in which one man in direct
relationship with one or more golden daffodils could
work redemption out for himself without involving the
daffodil. Shakespeare is more oriented toward society.

His heaven, or heaven on earth, is not peopled with lonely individuals wandering under lonely clouds. Instead it is a vibrant web of relationships between people: friends, couples, families, nations. Solution always comes from union; agony from separation. Disruption of the easy and orderly relationships among men, brings hell to earth, and tugs the city of man far from the city of God. The "nobleness of life" which Antony begins to sense, will draw man's city back again to God or gods. For the nobility of life comes from a proposition demanding such a doubly coupling phrase as "mutual pair" and such twinned unity as "twain." This way, the path of union is begun again. For Shakespeare, what was partial was but unresolved; with love came harmony. This was the binding and completing force of love, unknown to Rome. Redemption came when man loved man, was therefore joined to man.

Thus our first view of Antony, save for the words of Philo's speech, is not of him alone, but him and Cleopatra entering as a pair. And their embrace is fixed upon our mind, and kept there through the play. We know the play to be not Antony's alone, but their's, involving her. If harmony is to return to that which circumstance has split apart, then these two must at last embrace again to form their icon of an ideal world. And Enobarbus cannot die alone, for he and Antony make another kind of pair.

Yet the view, rather than the vision, of Antony and Cleopatra in embrace is not a simple one to comprehend.

> ... and our ills told us
> Is as our earing.

So Antony tells the messenger who comes to him from Rome. The lines are a kind of warning, or motto. In their implication they are as important for all other characters in the play as for Antony, or for us who listen. What do these lines mean? "Is as salutary to us as ploughing is to weed-grown fields"--so, dictionary-wise, the verb "to ere" becomes "to plough," and so

138

the glosses to the textbooks read. But: "is as our 'ear-ing" (pronounced cockney-like); "is as our hearing"; "is as we hear as ills, or hear them otherwise. " This equal-ly compelling definition is what investigation like that of Mr. Kökeritz helps us to recognize by re-tuning our ears. For what is in question is not only the consequence and harvests of ill-deeds, or their future prevention, but whether we hear them as ill-deeds at all, and can there-fore agree in their definition and hence in their conse-quence.

Antony later makes this problem clear to Caesar, when Antony says, "I learn you take things ill which are not so"; and though he adds, "or being, concern you not, " the second is subordinate to the first. For hearing goes on everywhere within the world, and what sounds one way when man hears in Rome, sounds otherwise when told in Egypt. Thus, understanding sways. Antony's own powers of hearing shift, as when in Egypt he begins a Roman thought, and listens with a Roman ear to his ill-deeds; or when in Rome his spirit wanders toward the Nile. Two sets of values strain the words he hears. Sometimes he hears through one, sometimes the other sets the key; and, each way, words seem different. An-tony duplicates the problem the world faces; or vice versa. What is important is that the world and Antony are shown to be alike. If Shakespeare's far-flung, swiftly-shifting scenes need any organic explanation for their prodigality, it can be found in their involvement of the world in a problem of ambiguity which might seem, otherwise, restricted and too personal. The problem, stripped of its variant metaphors, belongs to all.

The importance given by the circumstance that An-tony and Cleopatra are rulers, is of course that nothing they do can remain personal and fenced off. Their ac-tions obviously involve the world and the world's under-standing of what it hears. The point need not be labored. It speaks for itself, and has been said too often by oth-ers. What is more interesting to remember is that Shakespeare has shown the same kind of involvement, on a much smaller scale and with lesser characters, in

Romeo and Juliet. There, "fair Verona" splits apart.
Bickering between the servants of two families, spread
to the families, then involves the state. Personal grudges
can become, perhaps they are, state mutiny. Each party suffers equally. Two Capulets were lost; two Montagues; even the Prince has "lost a brace of kinsmen." The
play, as the prologue tells us, is not really about Romeo
and Juliet, but rather

> the continuance of their parents' rage,
> Which, but their children's end, nought could
> remove,
> Is now the two hours' traffic of our stage.

Although their deaths are referred to as "poor sacrifices
of our enmity," and the Prince urges a kind of reasonable
alliance between Capulets and Montagues, it is nevertheless the almost talismanic icon of the marriage that
brings the peace.

> O brother Montague! give me thy hand:
> This is my daughter's jointure, for no more
> Can I demand.

This joining of the parents' hands together in a twain or
mutual pair is more than carpentry of course, though
jointure will wed, or dowell, as in carpentry. As marriage jointure, it is also the estate settled in lieu of dow-
ry: the two families united as the children were; and
Verona, through this union, made a whole again.

The complexity of understanding has its part in
Romeo and Juliet too. What's in a name or word? How
do we hear them? Pure reason would make Juliet listen
as a Capulet. Romeo can never escape being in part a
Montague. But the conclusion of the play comes from no
rational sequence built on this or any reasonable ground;
instead it depends upon a recognition of the felt truth that
it is love that binds: the couple, families, and the state
alike.

In many ways, Antony and Cleopatra seems like a

rewriting of <u>Romeo and Juliet,</u> as though Shakespeare,
from the advantage, or perhaps more accurately the
confusion, of increased experience, were re-examining
the problem of disharmony and its resolution, pondering
the role of love.

Complexity in <u>Antony and Cleopatra</u> becomes, if I
am right, the very sense and substance of the play, its
strength and not its weakness. We are never permitted
to longer very long in one spot or with one point of view;
but we are never allowed, either, to forget where we have
been before. As we approach some sort of eventual simplicity of understanding, we realize that we have warrant
to approach it only because of the experience of complexity and the recognition of inter-dependencies. There are
a series of climactic events in the final scenes of <u>Antony
and Cleopatra,</u> on which to test our judgment. First is
the death of Enobarbus, then the death of Antony, and at
the end the death of Cleopatra. These are linked. Together they establish the definition and the involvements
of love, with a breadth of understanding and a density of
compassion which makes the solution of <u>Romeo and Juliet</u>
seem little more than a formula, though no less true for
all of that.

Let me, then test myself against these scenes. I
look at Enobarbus's death in this way. "O Antony!" he
cries; and at the end of this last speech, "O Antony!"
again, "O Antony!" This is his masculine pledge of loyalty, and with it re-ties bonds that slipped. Enobarbus's
departure had been the culminating symbol of the deser-
tion of old friends and soldiers, moved by discretion
rather than by their will. Reason may have shown Enobarbus, after his arrival in Caesar's camp, what happened to others who deserted to Caesar, but prudence would
have kept him there, had not his heart leaped up at Antony's "gentle adieus and greetings" sent loyally to him.
The quality of loyalty which Antony had shown was what
the Roman camp had lost, and Enobarbus missed it now.
So Enobarbus made an honorable act of heart; his suicide
became an act of love. Thus is love Platonized; and what
with Antony and Cleopatra has seemed only of the flesh,

here becomes spiritual instead. **Or,** as we later know: a
thing of fire and air, not earth and water save as purified.

Antony's own solitary state, alone, had changed by
what he did for his departed friend. What he gave Enobarbus, Enobarbus had returned to him. This spark of
loyalty had stayed in Antony. It was the opposite from
what we call a tragic flaw. It was instead the germ of new
nobility. Antony had known the words with which to speak
of nobleness of life, but had not known what really stood
up peerless in embrace. And that which crumbled him
since then, had been a weakness of his power to comprehend. Within him he had held the seed of what he wished;
he could not otherwise respond to her, or feel the thing
he lacked. But Antony was also Roman, and it was the
Roman Mars in him that Cleopatra craved, not an Egyptian likeness of herself. If these two stood up as a truly
peerless pair, it was because their union held both natures
bound in pair. Not a surrender of either: this would have
meant no mutual pair at all. Antony, alas, never made
the microcosmic effort, in these stages of his life, to balance contraries in himself; nor taught her how to do the
same. For, lusting hungrily, he only rushed to Cleopatra's arms. What happened was a doubling of herself; that
which was Roman he had cast aside. "Let Rome in Tiber
melt"; and so it does when life is carried out this way.
At least Rome melts in Antony, and he grows weak; while
Rome remains outside and wages war. Thus Antony, when
Hercules had left his heir, held little more than an Egyptian navy on his side to fight with him as ally; nor had Antony other than Eros as his fumbling armorer. And these
would not suffice to keep them peerless. Shrewdness like
Caesar's always conquers when the fight is so.

"It is difficult to care what happens to them," the reviewer of the play had said. "They only achieve the grandeur history suggests, when they begin to lose everything."
He might have been much wiser had he said that they a-
chieve their grandeur only when they had lost everything;
but "grandeur" has new meaning for us now. For what is
false and shallow has been swept away, and Antony could
settle on the issues thus made clear. Eros has killed

himself for Antony, as Enobarbus did; and Antony thinks
Cleopatra dead by her own hand. "My queen and Eros,"
Antony says:

> Have by their brave instruction got upon me
> A nobleness in record; but I will be
> A bridegroom in my death, and run into't
> As to a lover's bed.

This is a further definition of nobleness which does
not contradict the "nobleness of life," the proposition he
had felt at first, but it explains it as he did not know it
then. "Since Cleopatra died," he said to Eros, before
Eros killed himself, "I have lived in such dishonor, that
the gods detest my baseness." But what Antony felt was
base was his disloyalty to her, expressed by reason at
the expense of love. Dishonor finds its opposite in hon-
or; heaven is the opposite of base; a race, or root, of
heaven should breed gods. So Antony, like a bridegroom,
honoring her, unites with her in death. His purgatory of
experience is passed. This kind of bridegroom he had
never been before, nor had he used the word, nor run to
just this kind of married lover's bed. Marriage itself is
a symbolic alliance he had never felt, nor had he known
what really makes a mutual pair, contracted by their
love. His link to Octavia was made, instead, by purely
Roman virtues at their best. Reason and practicality
made the bond between himself and her, as between him
and Fulvia. Cleopatra had not been a wife before, only
the mistress of his flesh, a union with no standing in itself. Yet the Egyptian way held in it something which the
Roman way had lacked. True marriage sanctifies the
senses, but it starts with them. What was now needed
was to recognize the vows of loyalty which couples make:
to join, that is, with love and fix with honor. This is
true wedding; this, Antony now pledged; meaning his
word, as bridegroom, as he ran to her.
  As Enobarbus's death, and Eros's, joins them in
manly love for Antony; so Antony's death in turn joins
him to Cleopatra as a spouse. Thus groups begin to

form within the world again, where otherwise man only
stood alone. As Enobarbus seemed, dramatically, to
point attention toward Antony, that we might test if Antony were worthy of the pledge which Enobarbus made;
so Antony's vows direct us on to Cleopatra. She becomes
a test for both. For if Antony's love has been pledged to
an unworthy object, then he is wholly made the fool, and
Enobarbus has been foolish in his turn. How, then, will
Cleopatra understand and act, where will she turn when
her own moment of decision comes? And will we understand? "Not know me yet?"

"My desolation does begin to make a better life, " she
says. For she has had her purgatory, felt her own lone-
liness. "What poor an instrument, " she says, meaning
herself, "may do a noble deed. " Yet "none our parts so
poor, " she once had said, "but is a race of heaven. " So
be it now for her, giving new definition to the words. It
is a noble deed she seeks; nobility becomes important to
her too. She is resolved by Antony's witness what to do;
and those who think she later shrewdly toys with shifting
of her lot to Caesar's care, forget how shrewdly Roman
Cleopatra has become, though she will prove it in a nobler
way within herself. They have forgotten too, or did not
hear, what she replied when Antony said to her: "Of
Caesar seek your honor with your safety. " "They do not
go together, " Cleopatra cried. This was a paradox she
recognized; for honor at the first had seemed a purely
Roman word, but so did prudent safety too. And honor
now was only to be found when one pursued with daring,
not a Roman trait.

"Then is it sin, " she said to Charmion, when Antony
had died,

> To rush into the secret house of death,
> Ere death dare come to us? ...
> We'll bury him; and then, what's brave,
> what's <u>noble</u>,
> Let's do it after the high Roman fashion,
> And make death proud to take us.

ANTONY AND CLEOPATRA

If she spoke otherwise than this to Caesar later on, she
spoke with worn-out Roman words as they had been debased by Caesar's tongue: a lingua roma not to be be-
lieved by either side in such a dialogue. But Cleopatra
knew what words and deeds can really mean, and that to
link them was a marriage too. "Now Charmion, " Cleopatra says,

> Show me, my women, like a queen; go fetch
> My best attires; I am again for Cydnus,
> To meet Mark Antony.

And so she is again for Cydnus in her death. But not as
her own final words are proof, for Cydnus to repeat the
meaning of the scene as she and others understood it then,
but to begin again, to clarify what had been vague at first.

> Give me my robe, put on my crown; I have
> Immortal longings in me; ...

So she had always had, when she had known

> Eternity was in our lips and eyes,
> Bliss in our brows bent; none our parts so poor
> But was a race of heaven.

Now it was the union which counted; not Antony's kiss nor
the embrace of bodies, but the marriage which binds even
after death, and which she makes from death. "Husband,
I come, " she says; "now to that name my courage prove
my title!" Now--what significance the adverb has!--
when Cleopatra's words and deed unite, Shakespeare has
made of suicide what turns it to a proto-Christian sacra-
ment, joining the two as Romeo and Juliet had been joined together by the priest. The words of Cleopatra are
what modify the deed, and by her words we know her and
her final elements. Not earth and water: these were of
the Nile and bred the aspic which brought death; but "fire
and air; my other elements I give to baser life. "

In marriage she embraces all the bourgeois terms
and values she had seemed to scorn. And, in her, blos-
som all the states which woman has as a potential, no
matter what her rank. She is in her own words a milk-
maid, wife and mother of a babe, although she keeps her
status as a queen and Venus ("O eastern star, " that morning star), and fire and air, giving up earth and water as
mere flesh. It is in this complete and purifying way that
Cleopatra catches up all woman in herself. La donna e
mobile is not relevant at all, though critics sometimes
say so. What is all woman in her is her scope and her
capacity for love, and this amalgam she binds to her
"man of men. "

The marriage is the thing. This Dryden also knew,
for when he named his play All For Love, he took a
phrase that Shakespeare's time and his used for a posy
(the inscription) in a marriage or betrothal ring. Marriage requires the giving of a ring; it is the symbol of the
binding force, becomes a witness of the pact, when with
the ring one weds. Had Cleopatra earlier in the play received a ring from Antony as token of what "twain" meant
to him then, its posy might have read, as some rings in
Elizabethan times did read:

> Pity my passions.

This was what drew them then. Reason they cast aside.
But now, the wedding ring she would have worn, ready
and suited for it at the end, should be inscribed like this,
as some rings read in Shakespeare's day, to show what
Antony and Cleopatra learned:

> A pledge that binds
> Two hearts, two minds.

Our memory returns to Caesar at this point, and to
those words he said at Rome, when Lepidus and he and
Antony met:

ANTONY AND CLEOPATRA

> Yet, if I knew
> What hoop should hold us stanch, from
> edge to edge
> O' the world I would pursue it.

What he was talking of was what binds man to man, holds them together, keeps the world as one. "Give me leave, Caesar, " then Agrippa says at once; and thinking of the words that Caesar spoke, suggests Octavia as a wife for Antony. How little such a loveless bond would prove, the play goes on to show. Agrippa had not seen the vision Enobarbus wove for him; those words came later. Empire indeed had need of marriage, but the proper ring for it was such a golden hoop as Antony pursued to the world's edge, and which he found at last. Would Caesar understand, when at the end he gazed on Cleopatra in her death? Would we?

It was the amalgamation of seeming contraries of heart and mind that counted in the end to fill the lacks in each alone, and make a mutual pair. This was a twain to make a union firm; and they had learned to read what words contain, and what they spoke. And so, I hope, with Shakespeare's help, can we. For when the play began, this regal pair seemed inaccessible in height to us. Yet as these two were stripped down to our lot, we came to share and were involved with them. Their first words had remained superlatives. But in the end they carried no hyperbole. The pair had proved their right to share nobility, and by their deeds had proved at last these words as suitable. Sharing with them, the words can be ours too. The Roman time, and Shakespeare's, and our own complexly are alike and need their hoop. Shakespeare still speaks to us,

> ... and our ills told us
> Is as our earing.

147

NO